Home
Baking

cakes • cookies • pies • pastries • breads

Home Baking

This edition published in 2008 for Index Books Ltd

Parragon
Queen Street House
4 Queen Street
Bath BA1 IHE, UK

Copyright © Parragon Books Ltd 2007

This edition designed by Shelley Doyle
Cover designed by Talking Design
Cover photography by Mark Wood
Cover home economist Pamela Gwyther

ISBN 978-1-4075-2149-7

Printed in China

NOTES FOR THE READER

This book uses metric and imperial measurements. Follow the same units
of measurement throughout; do not mix metric and imperial. All spoon
measurements are level, unless otherwise stated: teaspoons are assumed to be
5ml and tablespoons are assumed to be 15ml. Unless otherwise stated, milk is
assumed to be whole, eggs and individual fruits such as bananas are medium,
and pepper is freshly ground black pepper.

Recipes using raw or very lightly cooked eggs should be avoided by children,
the elderly, pregnant women, convalescents and anyone suffering from an
illness.

Sufferers from nut allergies should be aware that some of the readymade
ingredients in the recipes in this book may contain nuts. Pregnant and breast-
feeding women are advised to avoid eating peanuts and peanut products.

Vegans should be aware that some of the ready-made ingredients in the
recipes in this book may be derived from animal products.

Vegetarians should be aware that some of the ready-made ingredients in the
recipes in this book may contain meat or meat products.

Contents

Introduction

Baking is just about the most satisfying type of cooking there is. Perhaps it's the aroma of fresh croissants as they emerge from the oven, the rewarding pleasure of cutting into a home-made Christmas cake or the comforting knowledge that a plate of irresistible brownies awaits the kids when they return from school. Whatever the reason, home baking is probably the world's best therapy as it always makes you feel good about yourself – and family and friends will share that opinion too.

From pies and tarts to muffins and biscuits and from simple sponge cakes to elaborate gateaux, this book is packed with recipes to suit all tastes and every occasion, whatever your level of skill, family budget and available time. You don't have to spend hours in the kitchen to whisk up a batch of tasty biscuits or savoury cheese scones that will easily surpass the store-bought varieties. Traditional Apple Pie (see page 28) is a quick, easy and inexpensive dessert that is the perfect end to Sunday lunch with the family, while those who have more time to lavish on preparing an elegant dinner party treat might like to delight their guests with a rich Dark & White Chocolate Torte (see page 136). There are also lots of recipes that look impressive but are astonishingly simple to make.

The recipes are divided into four main sections – Family Treats, Sweet Delights, Savoury Bites and Festive Feasts – making it simple to find exactly the right cake or bake that you need. However, you don't have to follow this demarcation slavishly. For example, while Lemon Meringue Pie (see page 32) is a great family favourite, it would also be a good choice for an informal supper party and there's no reason why you have to wait until Christmas to enjoy the deliciously moist gingerbread Lebkuchen (see page 162). Sun-dried Tomato Rolls (see page 100) would be as welcome in a picnic basket as they are on the dinner table, while Shortbread Fantails (see page 84) are equally good with morning coffee and with ice cream at the end of lunch. The final section of the book is the place to go for just such mix-and-match ideas. Four sub-sections – Morning Coffee with Friends, Afternoon Tea with the Family, Kids' Party Time and An Occasion to Impress – offer lots of helpful suggestions for these familiar occasions.

Essential equipment

Measuring: Accurate measurement of the ingredients is essential for success with home baking. Dry ingredients, such as flour and sugar, should be weighed precisely on kitchen scales. Liquids, such as water and milk, should be measured in a graduated jug. Small quantities of both liquid and dry ingredients, such as vanilla essence and grated lemon rind, should be measured in standard spoons.

Kitchen scales may be electronic, spring or balance. The first are quite expensive but extremely accurate. They usually have a switch for changing the read-out from metric to imperial measurements (both sets of measurements are given throughout this book). It is worth keeping spare batteries in stock. Spring scales are less expensive and very practical, although if the spring breaks it cannot be repaired. Dials usually indicate both metric and imperial measurements. Old-fashioned balance scales look lovely in a traditional kitchen but are not so easy to use or so convenient as other types. If you use both metric and imperial measures (though not in the same recipe), you will need to buy two sets of weights.

Measuring jugs may be made of plastic or glass and are usually heatproof, but do check. If they are clear, it is easier to see the level. Always measure at eye level. The jugs are usually graduated in both metric and imperial measurements.

A set, or better still, several sets of measuring spoons are invaluable as ordinary tableware is not standard in size. Sets usually consist of $1/4$, $1/2$ and 1 teaspoon, plus 1 tablespoon. Some also include $1/8$ teaspoon and $1/2$ tablespoon. Spoons with long handles are particularly useful for reaching inside spice jars. As with measuring dry ingredients in cups, spoons should be overfilled and then levelled with the blade of a knife.

Sifting: Even ready-sifted flours should be sifted again before use in fine baking. A medium or large bowl-shaped sieve with a fine mesh is suitable for sifting into a bowl and one with a lip that will rest on the rim is best. A smaller sieve – about 10 cm/4 in diameter – is useful for sifting small quantities of icing sugar and cocoa powder for decoration. You can use metal or nylon for most baking purposes but if you are sifting fruit to remove the seeds, for example, nylon is better as it doesn't react with the acid in the fruit.

A flour dredger is not essential but it does help to spread flour evenly on a work surface before pastry is rolled out. A sugar dredger is useful for sprinkling the tops of pies before or after baking. Make sure that the sugar crystals are brushed off the top of the container after refilling as you will find it impossible to unscrew the top again if they have stuck to the thread.

Mixing: Most kitchens contain a range of bowls and you can use glass, stainless steel, plastic, aluminium or earthenware for almost all baking purposes. However, neither plastic nor aluminium is suitable for whisking egg whites. Copper is the perfect choice for really successful meringue. A ceramic bowl is ideal for pastry as it helps to keep the mixture cold. Make sure you use a bowl of the appropriate size that allows plenty of room for stirring and/or beating.

Wooden spoons with curved and straight sides are invaluable, especially for stirring liquids while they are heating. The handles may be used for shaping biscuits while they are still warm from the oven.

A balloon whisk can be used for most whisking purposes and is very efficient. A flat whisk is helpful when whisking small quantities, such as an egg yolk glaze. A long, thin whisk will enable you to beat a mixture in a jug but is not essential.

An electric mixer, especially if it is supplied with dough hooks as well as whisks, saves time and effort.

A flexible spatula is the perfect tool for scraping cake batters out of the bowl and into a cake tin and for folding in beaten mixtures without destroying their aeration.

Pastry-making tools: Rolling pins may be made of metal, wood or marble. Both metal and marble help to keep the dough cold, but marble is extremely heavy. Plastic and glass rolling pins that can be filled with cold water are also available. Some designs have handles, some don't. It doesn't really matter which you choose, but if you tend to be heavy-handed, then a rolling pin with handles is probably a better choice.

You can roll out pastry on any smooth surface and a pastry board is not essential. However, a marble board does help to keep the dough cold and needs only light flouring.

A metal pastry blender is used to rub the fat into flour. It helps to keep the mixture cool, but many cooks prefer to use their fingertips.

A pastry brush is a useful, multi-purpose tool. It can be used for brushing glaze over a pie, brushing the edges of pastry before sticking them together and for brushing a tin with oil or melted butter to prevent the mixture from sticking.

A wide variety of cutters is available. Plain and fluted round cutters are perfect for tartlets and biscuits. It's worth buying a set of at least three different sizes. Cutters with handles produce a more even pressure. They may be made of plastic or metal. Plastic doesn't rust, but metal cutters are sharper and won't rust if thoroughly dried after washing. Novelty shapes, such as Christmas trees, hearts, gingerbread figures and moons, are also available. These are mainly used for biscuits.

A pastry wheel is useful for making a decorative edge when cutting out dough, particularly for lattice strips. You can also buy a lattice cutter, but this is far from essential.

Tins, dishes and trays: All the cake recipes in this book specify both size and shape of the tin. If you use a different size tin or a rectangular tin rather than a round one, the cake may not rise properly or may be disappointing in some other way. It is worth buying good-quality, heavy-gauge tins that will prevent scorching and will not distort. This is especially important for rich fruit cakes. They are available with a loose base to make it easier to remove the cake after baking. Non-stick linings are great for Victoria sponge tins, although they will still require greasing before use. They are also good for deeper light sponge cakes. A springform tin, with a clip that can be loosened for unmoulding the cake, saves a lot of worry if you are baking a fragile confection for a special occasion. Cake tins are available in a variety of shapes from ring moulds to hearts.

Bun trays, popover trays and muffin pans are useful for making small cakes and tartlets. Again it is worth buying good-quality cookware – non-stick if you like – which will last a lifetime. The size and number of the individual cups vary, so check the recipe before you start.

Loaf tins are rectangular and variable in size. They are available in a variety of materials and may be non-stick. Heavy-gauge, oxidised steel is very reliable.

Tart tins may be loose-based or solid. The former are used for tarts baked with a filling so that they can be lifted out easily. The latter are used for cooking the base, which is then turned out and left to cool. It can then be filled – still upside down – with fruit, whipped cream, etc. Both kinds of tin are available in different sizes and depths.

Pie dishes are traditionally ceramic and often very attractive. This material allows the heat to penetrate to the centre of the pie without the crust becoming overcooked. Make sure that the dish has a flat rim.

A heavy baking sheet is invaluable for meringues and biscuits as the heat is distributed quickly and evenly to produce a crisp result. Some have a lip on one long side, while others have a rim all the way around.

Other equipment: A palette knife is useful for smoothing the surface of cake batter and for applying and smoothing icing. Strong nylon icing bags with a selection of nozzles are necessary if you enjoy decorating cakes, although you can also make a disposable bag from a cone of greaseproof paper. A variety of other kitchen gadgets, such as a biscuit press, bird-shaped pie support or shortbread mould, while not essential, can be fun to have – put them on your birthday or wedding present list.

Pointers to perfection

Although, as with all cooking, some recipes are a little more demanding than others, baking – whether cakes, pies, savoury nibbles, bread or biscuits – is not particularly difficult. Certainly, the 'average' cook will find all the recipes in this book within his or her scope and even beginners will be able to master many of them more or less immediately. However, there are a few extra tips worth bearing in mind to avoid disappointment.

- Always read the recipe through and collect the measured ingredients together before you start cooking.

- Take care if you substitute ingredients as the substitute may seem similar but have different properties. In most cases, soft margarine, for example, cannot be successfully substituted for block margarine or butter.

- Preheat the oven to the specified temperature. This usually takes about 15 minutes and the recipe will indicate the appropriate stage in the method.

- Check the 'use-by' dates on store-cupboard ingredients, such as flour and nuts, which can go off over time.

- Don't cut corners to try to save time, as this will often end in failure. For example, a mixture may need to be chilled in the refrigerator to make it easier to roll out and handle and to guarantee a crisp texture when cooked. Similarly, if a pre-cooked filling needs to be completely cold before being topped with dough, leave plenty of time to avoid a soggy disappointment.

- Mix cake batters until they are just mixed – you will soon be able to recognise this point. If, for example, the flour is not completely folded into a whisked mixture, the dry pockets formed will cause the cake to crack during baking. Unfortunately, overmixing is likely to have the same result.

- Grease or grease and line a cake tin if the recipe specifies. However, if you use baking parchment, rather than greaseproof paper, greasing may not be necessary. Baking parchment is an especially good choice if you are baking meringue.

- Place whatever you are baking in the centre of a conventional oven, unless the recipe specifies otherwise. Avoid opening the door during cooking, especially if you are baking a delicate cake, which may be prone to collapse if exposed to a cold draught.

- Follow the instructions for cooling cakes and biscuits. Some should be turned out on to a wire cooling rack straight away, while others need to remain in the tin or on the baking sheet for a few minutes first to allow them to firm up slightly. Very rich cakes are often left to cool completely in the tin before unmoulding.

- Store cakes and biscuits in separate airtight containers. They will usually keep for a few days, although rich fruit cake can be stored for much longer. In the unlikely event of any cake being left over after it has been cut, wrap it in foil before returning to an airtight container. Cakes destined for decoration with fruit or cream should be stored undecorated or they will become soggy. They can be kept briefly in the refrigerator and served chilled or brought back to room temperature to serve.

- Finally, if things do go wrong, be imaginative. You will be surprised by what can be disguised with whipped cream and fresh or canned fruit. Cut off any sad pieces – sunken or burnt – and cover the remainder. Make the most of ready-to-roll icing, shredded coconut, icing sugar, chocolate sprinkles or whatever else seems a good idea. Cakes that have broken on unmoulding can be used as the basis for a delicious home-made trifle or stamped into shapes with biscuit cutters.

Family Treats

This chapter is packed with traditional favourites from classic British Bakewell Tart (see page 33) to the mouth-watering American Double Chocolate Brownies (see page 52). There's something for everyone from grandmas to toddlers, including plenty of lovely sticky desserts and cakes that will appeal to kids of all ages. The emphasis throughout is on fabulous flavour combined with ease of preparation. Even the children in the family will probably enjoy helping to make Fruity Flapjacks (see page 50) or Gingerbread People (see page 46). This is everyday baking at its best – it looks great, tastes wonderful and won't break the bank. But beware – you may well find that your home has become a scrumptious social centre for coffee mornings, after-school homework clubs, unexpected midweek guests, regular weekend visits from the extended family and old-fashioned tea parties. Of course, you'll never have any problems with leftovers.

Victoria Sandwich Cake

SERVES: 8

PREP: 10 MINS +
20 MINS
COOLING

COOKING: 25-30 MINS

Ingredients

175 g/6 oz butter, softened,
* plus extra for greasing*

175 g/6 oz self-raising flour

1 tsp baking powder

175 g/6 oz golden caster sugar

3 eggs

FILLING

3 tbsp raspberry jam

600 ml/1 pint double cream,
* whipped*

16 fresh strawberries, halved

caster sugar, for dusting

Preheat the oven to 180°C/350°F/Gas Mark 4, then grease and line the bases of 2 x 20-cm/8-inch sandwich tins. Sift the flour and baking powder into a bowl and add the butter, sugar and eggs. Mix together, then beat well until smooth.

Divide the mixture evenly between the prepared tins and smooth the surfaces. Bake in the preheated oven for 25-30 minutes, or until well risen and golden brown, and the cakes feel springy when lightly pressed.

Leave to cool in the tins for 5 minutes, then turn out and peel off the lining paper. Transfer to wire racks to cool completely. Sandwich the cakes together with the raspberry jam, whipped double cream and strawberry halves. Sprinkle the caster sugar on top and serve.

Carrot Cake

SERVES: 8

PREP: 15 MINS +
20 MINS
COOLING/
STANDING

COOKING: 1 HR 5 MINS

Ingredients

butter, for greasing

175 g/6 oz light muscovado sugar

3 eggs

175 ml/6 fl oz sunflower oil

175 g/6 oz coarsely grated carrots

2 ripe bananas, mashed

55 g/2 oz walnuts, chopped

280 g/10 oz plain flour

½ tsp salt

1 tsp bicarbonate of soda

2 tsp baking powder

FROSTING

200 g/7 oz cream cheese

½ tsp vanilla essence

115 g/4 oz icing sugar

25 g/1 oz walnuts, chopped

Preheat the oven to 180°C/350°F/Gas Mark 4. Grease and line the base of a 23-cm/9-inch springform cake tin. Place the sugar, eggs, sunflower oil, carrots, bananas and walnuts in a bowl. Sift in the flour, salt, bicarbonate of soda and baking powder. Beat the mixture until smooth.

Turn the mixture into the prepared tin and bake in the preheated oven for 1 hour 5 minutes, or until well risen and golden brown and a skewer inserted into the centre comes out clean. Leave in the tin for 10 minutes, then turn out and peel off the lining paper. Transfer to a wire rack to cool completely.

To make the frosting, place the cream cheese and vanilla essence in a bowl and beat well to soften. Beat in the icing sugar a tablespoon at a time, until smooth. Swirl over the cake and sprinkle the chopped walnuts on top. Leave in a cool place for the frosting to harden slightly before serving.

Coffee Streusel Cake

SERVES: 8

PREP: 50 MINS

COOKING: 1 HR

Ingredients

*100 g/3½ oz butter, melted and
cooled, plus extra for greasing*

275 g/9½ oz plain flour

1 tbsp baking powder

75 g/2¾ oz caster sugar

150 ml/5 fl oz milk

2 eggs

*2 tbsp instant coffee mixed with
1 tbsp boiling water*

50 g/1¾ oz almonds, chopped

icing sugar, for dusting

TOPPING

75 g/2¾ oz self-raising flour

75 g/2¾ oz demerara sugar

2 tbsp butter, diced

1 tsp ground mixed spice

1 tbsp water

Grease a 23-cm/9-inch loose-bottomed round cake tin with the butter and line with baking paper. Sieve the flour and baking powder together into a large mixing bowl, then stir in the caster sugar.

Whisk the milk, eggs, melted butter and coffee mixture together and pour on to the dry ingredients. Add the chopped almonds and mix lightly together. Spoon the mixture into the prepared tin.

To make the topping, mix the self-raising flour and demerara sugar together.

Rub in the butter with your fingertips until the mixture resembles breadcrumbs. Sprinkle in the mixed spice and water and bring the mixture together into loose crumbs. Sprinkle the topping evenly over the surface of the cake mixture in the tin.

Bake in a preheated oven, 190°C/375°F/Gas Mark 5, for about 1 hour. If the topping starts to brown too quickly, cover loosely with foil. Leave to cool in the tin. Turn out, dust with icing sugar and serve.

Mississippi Mud Cake

Ingredients

*250 g/9 oz butter, cut into pieces,
   plus extra for greasing*

150 g/5½ oz plain chocolate

425 g/15 oz golden caster sugar

250 ml/9 fl oz hot water

3 tbsp coffee liqueur or brandy

250 g/9 oz plain flour

1 tsp baking powder

25 g/1 oz cocoa powder

2 eggs, beaten

TO DECORATE

fresh raspberries

chocolate curls

Preheat the oven to 160°C/325°F/Gas Mark 3, then grease and line a 20-cm/8-inch round cake tin. Break the chocolate into pieces, then place the butter, chocolate, sugar, hot water and coffee liqueur in a large, heavy-based saucepan over a low heat and stir until the chocolate melts.

Stir until smooth, transfer the mixture to a large bowl and leave to cool for 15 minutes. Sift in the flour, baking powder and cocoa and whisk in, then whisk in the eggs. Pour the mixture into the prepared cake tin.

Bake in the preheated oven for 1½ hours, or until risen and firm to the touch. Leave to cool in the tin for 30 minutes, then turn out and peel off the lining paper. Transfer to a wire rack to cool completely. Decorate with fresh raspberries and chocolate curls and serve.

SERVES: 16

PREP: 25 MINS +
         30 MINS
         COOLING

COOKING: 1 HR 30 MINS

Preserved Ginger Cake

Ingredients

115 g/4 oz butter, plus extra
for greasing

225 g/8 oz self-raising flour

1 tbsp ground ginger

1 tsp ground cinnamon

½ tsp bicarbonate of soda

115 g/4 oz light muscovado sugar

grated rind of ½ lemon

2 eggs

1½ tbsp golden syrup

1½ tbsp milk

TOPPING

6 pieces of stem ginger, plus
4 tbsp ginger syrup from the jar

115 g/4 oz icing sugar

lemon juice

Preheat the oven to 160°C/325°F/Gas Mark 3. Grease and line the base of an 18-cm/7-inch square tin. Sift the flour, ginger, cinnamon and bicarbonate of soda into a bowl. Rub in the butter, then stir in the sugar and lemon rind. Make a well in the centre. Place the eggs, syrup and milk in a separate bowl and whisk together. Pour into the dry ingredients and beat until smooth.

Spoon the mixture into the prepared tin and bake in the preheated oven for 45-50 minutes, or until well risen and firm to the touch. Leave the cake to cool in the tin for 30 minutes, then turn out on to a wire rack and peel off the lining paper. Leave to cool completely.

To make the topping, cut each piece of stem ginger into quarters and arrange the pieces on top of the cake. Sift the icing sugar into a bowl and stir in the ginger syrup and enough lemon juice to make a smooth icing. Place the icing in a polythene bag and cut a tiny hole in one corner. Drizzle the icing over the cake. Leave to set, then cut the cake into squares and serve.

Rich Fruit Cake

SERVES: 12

PREP: 35 MINS +
1 HR
COOLING

COOKING: 1 HR 45 MINS

Ingredients

butter, for greasing

175 g/6 oz stoned unsweetened dates

125 g/4½ oz no-soak dried prunes

200 ml/7 fl oz unsweetened orange juice

2 tbsp black treacle

1 tsp finely grated lemon rind

1 tsp finely grated orange rind

225 g/8 oz wholemeal self-raising flour

1 tsp mixed spice

125 g/4½ oz seedless raisins

125 g/4½ oz golden sultanas

125 g/4½ oz currants

125 g/4½ oz dried cranberries

3 large eggs, separated

TO DECORATE

1 tbsp apricot jam, warmed

icing sugar, to dust

175 g/6 oz sugarpaste

strips of orange rind

Grease and line a deep 20.5-cm/8 inch round cake tin. Chop the dates and prunes and place in a pan. Pour over the orange juice and simmer for 10 minutes. Remove the pan from the heat and beat the fruit mixture until puréed. Add the treacle and rinds and set aside to cool.

Sift the flour and spice into a bowl, adding any bran that remains in the sieve. Add the dried fruits. When the date and prune mixture is cool, whisk in the egg yolks. In a clean bowl, whisk the egg whites until stiff. Spoon the fruit mixture into the dry ingredients and mix together.

Gently fold in the egg whites. Transfer to the prepared tin and bake in a preheated oven, 170°C/325°F/Gas Mark 3, for 1½ hours. Leave to cool in the tin.

Remove the cake from the tin and brush the top with jam. Dust the work surface with icing sugar and roll out the sugarpaste thinly. Lay the sugarpaste over the top of the cake and trim the edges. Decorate with orange and lemon rind.

Blueberry & Lemon Drizzle Cake

SERVES: 12

PREP: 20 MINS +
30 MINS
COOLING

COOKING: 1 HR

Ingredients

225 g/8 oz butter, softened, plus
  extra for greasing

225 g/8 oz golden caster sugar

4 eggs, beaten

250 g/9 oz self-raising flour, sifted

finely grated rind and juice of
  1 lemon

25 g/1 oz ground almonds

200 g/7 oz fresh blueberries

TOPPING

juice of 2 lemons

115 g/4 oz golden caster sugar

Preheat the oven to 180°C/350°F/Gas Mark 4, then grease and line the base of a 20-cm/8-inch square cake tin. Place the butter and sugar in a bowl and beat together until light and fluffy. Gradually beat in the eggs, adding a little flour towards the end to prevent curdling. Beat in the lemon rind, then fold in the remaining flour and almonds with enough of the lemon juice to give a good dropping consistency.

Fold in three-quarters of the blueberries and turn into the prepared tin. Smooth the surface, then scatter the remaining blueberries on top. Bake in the preheated oven for 1 hour, or until firm to the touch and a skewer inserted into the centre comes out clean.

To make the topping, place the lemon juice and sugar in a bowl and mix together. As soon as the cake comes out of the oven, prick it all over with a fine skewer and pour over the lemon mixture. Leave to cool in the tin until completely cold, then cut into 12 squares to serve.

Almond & Hazelnut Gâteau

SERVES: 8

PREP: 1 HR +
1 HR 40 MINS
COOLING/
CHILLING

COOKING: 25 MINS

Ingredients

butter, for greasing

4 eggs

100 g/3½ oz caster sugar

50 g/1¾ oz ground almonds

50 g/1¾ oz ground hazelnuts

5½ tbsp plain flour

50 g/1¾ oz flaked almonds

icing sugar, for dusting

FILLING

100 g/3½ oz plain chocolate

1 tbsp butter

300 ml/10 fl oz double cream

Preheat the oven to190°C/375°F/Gas Mark 5. Grease and line the bases of 2 x 18-cm/7-inch round sandwich tins.

Whisk the eggs and caster sugar together for 10 minutes, or until very light and foamy and the whisk leaves a trail that lasts a few seconds when lifted.

Fold in the ground almonds and hazelnuts, sift the flour and fold in with a metal spoon or spatula. Pour into the prepared tins.

Sprinkle the flaked almonds over the top of one of the cakes, then bake both cakes in the preheated oven for 15-20 minutes, or until springy to the touch.

Leave to cool in the tins for 5 minutes, then turn out on to wire racks to cool completely.

To make the filling, melt the chocolate, remove from the heat and stir in the butter. Cool. Whip the cream until holding its shape, then fold in the chocolate until mixed.

Place the cake without the extra almonds on a serving plate and spread the filling over it. Leave to set slightly, then place the almond-topped cake on top of the filling and leave to chill in the refrigerator for 1 hour. Dust with icing sugar and serve.

Traditional Apple Pie

Ingredients

*750 g-1 kg/1 lb 10 oz-2 lb 4 oz
cooking apples, peeled, cored
and sliced*

*125 g/4½ oz soft light brown or
caster sugar, plus extra for
sprinkling*

*½-1 tsp ground cinnamon,
mixed spice or ground ginger*

1-2 tbsp water

PASTRY

350 g/12 oz plain flour

pinch of salt

6 tbsp butter or margarine

85 g/3 oz lard or white vegetable fat

about 6 tbsp cold water

beaten egg or milk, for glazing

To make the pastry, sift the flour and salt into a mixing bowl. Add the butter and fat and rub in with the fingertips until the mixture resembles fine breadcrumbs. Add the water and gather the mixture together into a dough. Wrap the dough and leave to chill for 30 minutes.

Preheat the oven to 220°C/425°F/Gas Mark 7. Roll out almost two-thirds of the pastry thinly and use to line a 20-23-cm/8–9-inch deep pie plate or shallow pie tin.

Mix the apples with the sugar and spice and pack into the pastry case; the filling can come up above the rim. Add the water if liked, particularly if the apples are a dry variety.

Roll out the remaining pastry to form a lid. Dampen the edges of the pie rim with water and position the lid, pressing the edges firmly together. Trim and crimp the edges.

Use the trimmings to cut out leaves or other shapes to decorate the top of the pie, dampen and attach. Glaze the top of the pie with beaten egg or milk, make 1-2 slits in the top and put the pie on a baking sheet.

Bake in the preheated oven for 20 minutes, then reduce the temperature to 180°C/350°F/ Gas Mark 4 and cook for about 30 minutes, until the pastry is a light golden brown. Serve hot or cold, sprinkled with sugar.

Apple & Blackberry Crumble

SERVES: 4

PREP: 15 MINS

COOKING: 40-45 MINS

Ingredients

900 g/2 lb cooking apples,
 peeled and sliced

300 g/10½ oz blackberries,
 fresh or frozen

55 g/2 oz light muscovado sugar

1 tsp ground cinnamon

custard or pouring cream, to serve

CRUMBLE

85 g/3 oz self-raising flour

85 g/3 oz plain wholemeal flour

115 g/4 oz butter

55 g/2 oz demerara sugar

Preheat the oven to 200°C/400°F/Gas Mark 6.
Peel and core the apples and cut into chunks. Place in
a bowl with the blackberries, sugar and cinnamon
and mix together, then transfer to an ovenproof
baking dish.

To make the crumble, sift the self-raising flour into a
bowl and stir in the wholemeal flour. Add the butter
and rub in with your fingers until the mixture
resembles coarse breadcrumbs. Stir in the sugar.

Spread the crumble over the apples and bake in the
preheated oven for 40-45 minutes, or until the apples
are soft and the crumble is golden brown and crisp.
Serve with custard or pouring cream.

Sticky Toffee Pudding

Ingredients

PUDDING

75 g/2¾ oz sultanas

150 g/5½ oz stoned dates, chopped

1 tsp bicarbonate of soda

2 tbsp butter, plus extra for greasing

200 g/7 oz brown sugar

2 eggs

200 g/7 oz self-raising flour, sifted

STICKY TOFFEE SAUCE

2 tbsp butter

175 ml/6 fl oz double cream

200 g/7 oz brown sugar

zested orange rind, to decorate

freshly whipped cream, to serve

To make the pudding, put the fruits and bicarbonate of soda into a heatproof bowl. Cover with boiling water and leave to soak.

Preheat the oven to 180°C/350°F/Gas Mark 4. Grease a round cake tin, 20 cm/8 inches in diameter, with butter. Put the remaining butter in a separate bowl, add the sugar and mix well. Beat in the eggs then fold in the flour. Drain the soaked fruits, add to the bowl and mix. Spoon the mixture evenly into the prepared cake tin. Transfer to the preheated oven and bake for 35-40 minutes. The pudding is cooked when a skewer inserted into the centre comes out clean. About 5 minutes before the end of the cooking time, make the sauce. Melt the butter in a saucepan over a medium heat. Stir in the cream and sugar and bring to the boil, stirring constantly. Lower the heat and simmer for 5 minutes.

Turn out the pudding onto a serving plate and pour over the sauce. Decorate with zested orange rind and serve with whipped cream.

Jam Roly Poly

Ingredients

175 g/6 oz self-raising flour, plus extra for dusting

pinch of salt

75 g/2¾ oz shredded suet

3-4 tbsp hot water

6 tbsp raspberry jam

2 tbsp milk

1 tbsp butter, for greasing

raspberries, to decorate

custard, to serve

Put the flour and salt into a bowl and mix together well. Add the suet, then stir in enough hot water to make a light dough. Using your hands, shape the dough into a ball. Turn out the dough onto a lightly floured work surface and knead gently until smooth. Roll out into a rectangle about 28 cm/11 inches x 23 cm/9 inches.

Spread the jam over the dough, leaving a border of about 1 cm/½ inch all round. Brush the border with milk. Starting with the short side, roll up the dough evenly until you have one large roll.

Lightly grease a large piece of aluminium foil with butter, then place the dough roll in the centre. Gently close up the foil around the dough, allowing room for expansion, and seal tightly. Transfer to a steamer on top of a pan of boiling water. Steam for about 1½ hours until cooked, topping up the water level when necessary.

Turn out the roly poly onto a serving platter and decorate with raspberries. Serve with hot custard.

Lemon Meringue Pie

Ingredients

PASTRY

200 g/7 oz plain flour, plus extra for dusting

100 g/3½ oz butter, diced, plus extra for greasing

50 g/1¾ oz icing sugar, sifted

finely grated rind of 1 lemon

1 egg yolk, beaten

3 tbsp milk

FILLING

3 tbsp cornflour

300 ml/10 fl oz cold water

juice and grated rind of 2 lemons

175 g/6 oz caster sugar

2 eggs, separated

To make the pastry, sift the flour into a bowl and rub in the butter. Mix in the remaining ingredients. Knead briefly on a lightly floured work surface. Leave to rest for 30 minutes. Preheat the oven to 180°C/350°F/ Gas Mark 4. Grease a 20-cm/8-inch ovenproof pie dish with butter. Roll out the pastry to a thickness of 5 mm/¼ inch and use it to line the dish. Prick with a fork, line with baking paper and fill with baking beans. Bake for 15 minutes. Remove from the oven. Lower the temperature to 150°C/300°F/Gas Mark 2.

To make the filling, mix the cornflour with a little water. Put the remaining water into a pan. Stir in the lemon juice and rind and cornflour paste. Bring to the boil, stirring. Cook for 2 minutes. Cool a little. Stir in 5 tablespoons of sugar and the egg yolks and pour into the pastry shell. In a separate bowl, whisk the egg whites until stiff. Gradually whisk in the remaining sugar and spread over the pie. Bake for 40 minutes. Remove from the oven and serve.

Bakewell Tart

SERVES: 4

PREP: 20 MINS +
30 MINS
RESTING

COOKING: 40 MINS

Ingredients

PASTRY

200 g/7 oz plain flour, plus extra
for dusting

100 g/3½ oz butter, diced, plus
extra for greasing

50 g/1¾ oz icing sugar, sifted

finely grated rind of 1 lemon

1 egg yolk, beaten

3 tbsp milk

4 tbsp strawberry jam

FILLING

100 g/3½ oz butter

100 g/3½ oz brown sugar

2 eggs, beaten

1 tsp almond essence

75 g/2¾ oz ground rice

3 tbsp ground almonds

3 tbsp flaked almonds, toasted

icing sugar, to dust

To make the pastry, sift the flour into a bowl. Rub in the butter. Mix in the icing sugar, lemon rind, egg yolk and milk. Knead briefly on a lightly floured work surface. Leave to rest for 30 minutes.

Preheat the oven to 190°C/375°F/Gas Mark 5. Grease a 20-cm/8-inch ovenproof flan tin with butter. Roll out the pastry to a thickness of 5 mm/¼ inch and use it to line the base and sides of the tin. Prick all over the base with a fork, then spread with jam.

To make the filling, cream together the butter and sugar until fluffy. Gradually beat in the eggs, followed by the almond essence, ground rice and ground almonds. Spread the mixture evenly over the jam-covered pastry, then scatter over the flaked almonds. Bake in the preheated oven for 40 minutes, until golden. Remove from the oven, dust with icing sugar and serve.

33

MAKES: 11

PREP: 15 MINS

COOKING: 12-15 MINS

Dried Cherry Cheesecake Muffins

Ingredients

150 g/5½ oz butter, plus extra
  for greasing

200 g/7 oz cream cheese

150 g/5½ oz caster sugar

3 large eggs, lightly beaten

300 g/10½ oz self-raising flour

100 g/3½ oz dried cherries,
  chopped

icing sugar, for dusting

Preheat the oven to 180°C/350°F/Gas Mark 4. Grease a deep 12-cup muffin tin.

Melt the butter and leave to cool slightly. In a large bowl, whisk the cream cheese and sugar together, add the eggs one at a time until well combined and then stir in the melted butter.

Mix the flour and cherries together in a bowl, then stir gently into the batter. Spoon into the prepared muffin tin, filling each hole to about two-thirds full, and bake for 12-15 minutes, or until golden brown. Remove from the oven and cool on a wire rack. Eat warm or cold, dusted lightly with icing sugar.

Triple Chocolate Muffins

Ingredients

250 g/9 oz plain flour

25 g/1 oz cocoa powder

2 tsp baking powder

½ tsp bicarbonate of soda

100 g/3½ oz plain chocolate chips

100 g/3½ oz white chocolate chips

2 eggs, beaten

300 ml/10 fl oz soured cream

85 g/3 oz light muscovado sugar

85 g/3 oz butter, melted

Preheat the oven to 200°C/400°F/Gas Mark 6.
Line 11 holes of 1 or 2 muffin trays with paper muffin
cases. Sift the flour, cocoa powder, baking powder and
bicarbonate of soda into a large bowl, add the plain
and white chocolate chips and stir.

Place the eggs, soured cream, sugar and butter in a
separate bowl and mix. Add the wet ingredients to the
dry ingredients and stir gently until just combined.

Using 2 forks, divide the mixture between the paper
cases and bake in the preheated oven for 20 minutes,
or until well risen and firm to the touch. Serve warm
or cold.

Apple & Cinnamon Muffins

MAKES: 6

PREP: 15 MINS

COOKING: 20-25 MINS

Ingredients

85 g/3 oz plain wholemeal flour

70 g/2½ oz plain white flour

1½ tsp baking powder

pinch of salt

1 tsp ground cinnamon

40 g/1½ oz golden caster sugar

2 small eating apples, peeled, cored and finely chopped

125 ml/4 fl oz milk

1 egg, beaten

55 g/2 oz butter, melted

TOPPING

12 brown sugar cubes, roughly crushed

½ tsp ground cinnamon

Preheat the oven to 200°C/400°F/Gas Mark 6. Line 6 holes of a muffin tray with paper muffin cases.

Sift the 2 flours, baking powder, salt and cinnamon into a large bowl and stir in the sugar and chopped apples. Place the milk, egg and butter in a separate bowl and mix. Add the wet ingredients to the dry ingredients and gently stir until just combined.

Divide the mixture between the paper cases. To make the topping, mix together the crushed sugar cubes and cinnamon and sprinkle over the muffins. Bake in the preheated oven for 20-25 minutes, or until risen and golden. Serve the muffins warm or cold.

Classic Oatmeal Cookies

MAKES: 30

PREP: 10 MINS

COOKING: 15 MINS

Ingredients

*175 g/6 oz butter or margarine,
plus extra for greasing*

275 g/9½ oz demerara sugar

1 egg

4 tbsp water

1 tsp vanilla essence

375 g/13 oz rolled oats

140 g/5 oz plain flour

1 tsp salt

½ tsp bicarbonate of soda

Preheat the oven to 350°F/180°C/Gas Mark 4 and grease a large baking sheet.

Cream the butter (or margarine, if using) and sugar together in a large mixing bowl. Beat in the egg, water and vanilla until the mixture is smooth.

In a separate bowl, mix the oats, flour, salt and bicarbonate of soda. Gradually stir the oat mixture into the butter mixture until thoroughly combined.

Put 30 rounded tablespoonfuls of cookie mixture onto the greased baking sheet, making sure they are well spaced. Transfer to the preheated oven and bake for 15 minutes, or until the cookies are golden brown.

Remove the cookies from the oven and place on a wire rack to cool before serving.

Peanut Butter Cookies

Ingredients

115 g/4 oz butter, softened, plus extra for greasing

115 g/4 oz crunchy peanut butter

115 g/4 oz golden caster sugar

115 g/4 oz light muscovado sugar

1 egg, beaten

½ tsp vanilla essence

85 g/3 oz plain flour

½ tsp bicarbonate of soda

½ tsp baking powder

pinch of salt

115 g/4 oz rolled oats

Preheat the oven to 180°C/350°F/Gas Mark 4, then grease 3 baking sheets. Place the butter and peanut butter in a bowl and beat together. Beat in the caster and muscovado sugars, then gradually beat in the egg and vanilla essence.

Sift the flour, bicarbonate of soda, baking powder and salt into the bowl and stir in the oats. Drop spoonfuls of the mixture on to the prepared baking sheets, spaced well apart to allow for spreading. Flatten slightly with a fork.

Bake in the preheated oven for 12 minutes, or until lightly browned. Leave to cool on the baking sheets for 2 minutes, then transfer to wire racks to cool completely.

MAKES: 30

PREP: 12 MINS

COOKING: 10 MINS

Cherry & Walnut Cookies

Ingredients

*175 g/6 oz butter or margarine,
plus extra for greasing*

200 g/7 oz light muscovado sugar

2 eggs

315 g/11¼ oz plain flour

pinch of salt

2 tsp baking powder

2 tbsp milk

1 tsp almond essence

150 g/4½ oz chopped walnuts

75 g/2¾ oz raisins

75 g/2¾ oz sultanas

75 g/2¾ oz maraschino cherries

350 g/12 oz wheat flakes, crushed

*15 maraschino cherries, cut in half
(optional)*

Preheat the oven to 190°C/375°F/Gas Mark 5. Grease a large baking sheet, cut cherries in half.

Cream the butter and sugar in a large mixing bowl until a fluffy consistency is reached. Beat in the eggs.

Gradually sift the flour, salt and baking powder into the creamed mixture. Add the milk and almond essence and mix thoroughly. Stir in the walnuts and dried fruit and mix well.

Form the dough into 30 or so balls (about 1 rounded tablespoon each) and roll in the crushed wheat flakes. Space the dough balls about 2 cm/1 inch apart on the greased baking sheet. Place half a maraschino cherry on the top of each dough ball, if desired. Transfer to the preheated oven and cook for 10 minutes, or until the cookies are light brown.

Transfer from the oven to a wire rack and let them cool.

MAKES: 30

PREP: 10 MINS

COOKING: 20 MINS

Gingernuts

Ingredients

125 g/4½ oz butter, plus extra
  for greasing

350 g/12 oz self-raising flour

pinch of salt

200 g/7 oz caster sugar

1 tbsp ground ginger

1 tsp bicarbonate of soda

75 g/2¾ oz golden syrup

1 egg, beaten

1 tsp grated orange rind

Lightly grease several baking trays with a little butter.

Sieve the flour, salt, sugar, ginger and bicarbonate of soda into a large mixing bowl.

Heat the butter and golden syrup together in a saucepan over a very low heat until the butter has melted.

Remove the pan from the heat and leave the butter and syrup mixture to cool slightly, then pour it on to the dry ingredients.

Add the egg and orange rind and mix thoroughly to a dough.

Using your hands, carefully shape the dough into 30 even-size balls.

Place the balls well apart on the prepared baking trays, then flatten them slightly with your fingers.

Bake in a preheated oven, 160°C/325°F/Gas Mark 3, for 15-20 minutes, then carefully transfer the biscuits to a wire rack to cool.

Chocolate Drop Cookies

MAKES: 20

PREP: 10 MINS

COOKING: 15-20 MINS

Ingredients

115 g/4 oz butter, plus extra
  for greasing

90 g/3¼ oz plain flour

2 tbsp cocoa powder

55 g/2 oz caster sugar

½ tsp vanilla essence

Preheat the oven to 190°C/375°F/Gas Mark 5. Grease 2-3 large baking sheets. Sift the flour and cocoa together.

Beat the butter, caster sugar and vanilla essence together in a large bowl until soft and fluffy. Stir in the flour mixture until well blended.

Drop teaspoonfuls of the mixture on to the prepared baking sheets, allowing room for the cookies to spread during cooking.

Bake the cookies in the preheated oven for 15-20 minutes, until firm. Leave for 1 minute, then transfer to a wire rack and leave to cool.

MAKES: 20, USING
LARGE CUTTERS

PREP: 30 MINS +
30 MINS
COOLING

COOKING: 15-20 MINS

Gingerbread People

Ingredients

115 g/4 oz butter, plus extra
for greasing

450 g/1 lb plain flour, plus extra
for dusting

2 tsp ground ginger

1 tsp mixed spice

2 tsp bicarbonate of soda

100 g/3½ oz golden syrup

115 g/4 oz light muscovado sugar

1 egg, beaten

TO DECORATE

currants

glacé cherries

85 g/3 oz icing sugar

3-4 tsp water

Preheat the oven to 160°C/325°F/Gas Mark 3, then grease 3 large baking sheets. Sift the flour, ginger, mixed spice and bicarbonate of soda into a large bowl. Place the butter, syrup and sugar in a saucepan over a low heat and stir until melted. Pour on to the dry ingredients and add the egg. Mix together to make a dough. The dough will be sticky to begin with, but will become firmer as it cools.

On a lightly floured work surface, roll out the dough to about 3 mm/⅛ inch thick and stamp out gingerbread people shapes. Place on the prepared baking sheets. Re-knead and re-roll the trimmings and cut out more shapes until the dough is used up. Decorate with currants for eyes and pieces of cherry for mouths. Bake in the oven for 15-20 minutes, or until firm and lightly browned.

Remove from the oven and leave to cool on the baking sheets for a few minutes, then transfer to wire racks to cool completely. Mix the icing sugar with the water to a thick consistency. Place the icing in a small polythene bag and cut a tiny hole in one corner. Pipe buttons or clothes shapes on to the cooled biscuits.

Lemon Butterfly Cakes

MAKES: 12

PREP: 20 MINS +
30 MINS
COOLING

COOKING: 15-20 MINS

Ingredients

115 g/4 oz self-raising flour

½ tsp baking powder

115 g/4 oz butter, softened

115 g/4 oz golden caster sugar

2 eggs, beaten

finely grated rind of ½ lemon

2-4 tbsp milk

icing sugar, for dusting

FILLING

55 g/2 oz butter

115 g/4 oz icing sugar

1 tbsp lemon juice

Preheat the oven to 190°C/375°F/Gas Mark 5. Place 12 paper cases in a bun tin. Sift the flour and baking powder into a bowl. Add the butter, sugar, eggs, lemon rind and enough milk to give a medium-soft consistency. Beat the mixture thoroughly until smooth, then divide between the paper cases and bake in the preheated oven for 15-20 minutes, or until well risen and golden. Transfer to wire racks to cool.

To make the filling, place the butter in a bowl. Sift in the icing sugar and add the lemon juice. Beat well until smooth and creamy. When the cakes are quite cold, use a sharp-pointed vegetable knife to cut a circle from the top of each cake, then cut each circle in half.

Spoon a little buttercream into the centre of each cake and press the 2 semi-circular pieces into it to resemble wings. Dust the cakes with sifted icing sugar before serving.

Fruity Flapjacks

Ingredients

sunflower oil, for brushing

140 g/5 oz rolled oats

115 g/4 oz demerara sugar

85 g/3 oz raisins

*115 g/4 oz low-fat sunflower
  margarine, melted*

Preheat the oven to 190°C/375°F/Gas Mark 5. Lightly brush a 28 x 18-cm/11 x 7-inch shallow rectangular cake tin with oil. Combine the oats, sugar and raisins with the margarine, stirring well.

Spoon the oat mixture into the tin and press down firmly with the back of a spoon. Bake in the preheated oven for 15-20 minutes, or until golden.

Using a sharp knife, score lines to mark out 14 bars, then leave the flapjack to cool in the tin for 10 minutes. Carefully transfer the bars to a wire rack to cool completely.

Chocolate Chip Flapjacks

MAKES: 12

PREP: 40 MINS

COOKING: 40 MINS

Ingredients

115 g/4 oz butter, plus extra
  for greasing

60 g/2¼ oz caster sugar

1 tbsp golden syrup

350 g/12 oz rolled oats

85 g/3 oz plain chocolate chips

85 g/3 oz sultanas

Preheat the oven to 180°C/350°F/Gas Mark 4. Lightly grease a shallow 20-cm/8-inch square cake tin.

Place the butter, caster sugar and golden syrup in a saucepan and cook over a low heat, stirring constantly until the butter and sugar melt and the mixture is well combined.

Remove the saucepan from the heat and stir in the rolled oats until they are well coated. Add the chocolate chips and the sultanas and mix well to combine everything.

Turn into the prepared tin and press down well.

Bake in the preheated oven for 30 minutes. Cool slightly, then mark into fingers. When almost cold, cut into bars or squares and transfer to a wire rack to cool completely.

Double Chocolate Brownies

Ingredients

115 g/4 oz butter, plus extra
for greasing

115 g/4 oz plain chocolate, broken
into pieces

300 g/10½ oz golden caster sugar

pinch of salt

1 tsp vanilla essence

2 large eggs

140 g/5 oz plain flour

2 tbsp cocoa powder

100 g/3½ oz white chocolate chips

FUDGE SAUCE

4 tbsp butter

225 g/8 oz golden caster sugar

150 ml/5 fl oz milk

250 ml/9 fl oz double cream

225 g/8 oz golden syrup

200 g/7 oz plain chocolate,
broken into pieces

Preheat the oven to 180°C/350°F/Gas Mark 4. Grease and line the bottom of a 18-cm/7-inch square cake tin. Place the butter and chocolate in a small heatproof bowl set over a saucepan of gently simmering water until melted. Stir until smooth. Leave to cool slightly. Stir in the sugar, salt and vanilla essence. Add the eggs, one at a time, until blended.

Sift the flour and cocoa powder into the mixture and beat until smooth. Stir in the chocolate chips, then pour the mixture into the tin. Bake in the preheated oven for 35-40 minutes, or until the top is evenly coloured and a cocktail stick inserted into the centre comes out almost clean. Leave to cool slightly while preparing the sauce.

To make the sauce, place the butter, sugar, milk, cream and syrup in a small saucepan and heat gently until the sugar has dissolved. Bring to the boil and stir for 10 minutes, or until the mixture is caramel-coloured. Remove from the heat and add the chocolate. Stir until smooth. Cut the brownies into squares and serve immediately with the sauce.

Hazelnut Squares

Ingredients

100 g/3½ oz butter, cut into small
  pieces, plus extra for greasing

150 g/5½ oz plain flour

salt

1 tsp baking powder

150 g/5½ oz soft brown sugar

1 egg, beaten

4 tbsp milk

100 g/3½ oz hazelnuts, halved

demerara sugar, for sprinkling
  (optional)

Preheat the oven to 180°C/350°F/Gas Mark 4. Grease
a 23-cm/9-inch square cake tin and line the base with
baking paper. Sift the flour, a pinch of salt and the
baking powder into a large bowl. Add the butter and
rub it in with your fingertips until the mixture
resembles fine breadcrumbs. Add the soft brown sugar
and stir to mix.

Add the beaten egg, milk and halved hazelnuts to the
dry ingredients and stir well until thoroughly combined
and the mixture is a soft consistency.

Spoon the mixture into the prepared cake tin and
smooth the surface. Sprinkle with demerara sugar,
if using. Bake in the preheated oven for 25 minutes,
or until the mixture is firm to the touch when pressed
with a finger. Leave to cool in the tin for 10 minutes,
then loosen the edges with a round-bladed knife and
turn out on to a wire rack to cool completely.
Cut into squares.

Cappuccino Squares

Ingredients

225 g/8 oz butter, softened, plus extra for greasing

225 g/8 oz self-raising flour

1 tsp baking powder

1 tsp cocoa powder, plus extra for dusting

225 g/8 oz golden caster sugar

4 eggs, beaten

3 tbsp instant coffee powder dissolved in 2 tbsp hot water

ICING

115 g/4 oz white chocolate, broken into pieces

4 tbsp butter, softened

3 tbsp milk

175 g/6 oz icing sugar

cocoa powder, to decorate

Preheat the oven to 180°C/350°F/Gas Mark 4. Grease and line the bottom of a shallow oblong 28 x 18-cm/11 x 7-inch tin. Sift the flour, baking powder and cocoa into a bowl. Add the butter, caster sugar, eggs and coffee. Beat well, by hand or with an electric whisk, until smooth. Spoon into the tin and smooth the top.

Bake in the preheated oven for 35-40 minutes, or until risen and firm. Leave to cool in the tin for 10 minutes, then turn out on to a wire rack and peel off the lining paper. Leave to cool completely. To make the icing, place the chocolate, butter and milk in a heatproof bowl set over a saucepan of simmering water and stir until the chocolate has melted.

Remove the bowl from the saucepan and sift in the icing sugar. Beat until smooth, then spread over the cake. Dust the top of the cake with sifted cocoa, then cut into squares.

Sweet Delights

Had a bad day and need something to cheer you up?

Had a good day and feel like celebrating? Either way, you need look no

further as this chapter is packed with delectable treats to provide comfort

or add sparkle. Recipes for tarts and pies, little cakes and rich desserts,

bars and biscuits all vie with each other to tempt your taste buds, satisfy

your sweet tooth and make every day seem special. They are ideal too for

home-baked gifts – always a joy to receive – or for that most competitive

of activities, the school cake sale. You don't have to be an expert to create

the simple elegance of Tarte au Citron (see page 58), the self-indulgent

luxury of Chocolate Fudge Cake (see page 74), the satisfying stickiness of

Chelsea Buns (see page 77) or the more-ish scrumptiousness of

Chewy Golden Cookies (see page 90).

Go on, spoil yourself.

Tarte Au Citron

SERVES: 6

PREP: 20 MINS +
15 MINS
COOLING

COOKING: 40-55 MINS

Ingredients

butter, for greasing

plain flour, for dusting

1 quantity Pâte Sucrée

FILLING

1 large egg

4 large egg yolks

140 g/5 oz golden caster sugar

*finely grated rind and juice
of 4 lemons (the juice should
measure 150 ml/5 fl oz)*

150 ml/5 fl oz double cream

icing sugar, for dusting

Preheat the oven to 200°C/400°F/Gas Mark 6, then grease a 23-cm/9-inch tart tin. On a lightly floured work surface, roll out the pastry and use it to line the tart tin, then bake blind. Reduce the oven temperature to 160°C/325°F/Gas Mark 3 and place a baking sheet in the oven.

To make the filling, place the egg, egg yolks and sugar in a bowl and whisk until smooth. Gently stir in the lemon rind, lemon juice and cream. Pour most of the filling into the pastry case, then place the tart tin on the preheated baking sheet in the oven and spoon in the rest of the filling.

Bake in the oven for 25-30 minutes, or until there is no sign of liquid movement in the filling. Leave to cool in the tin for 15 minutes and serve warm or chilled. Before serving, sift over the icing sugar to dust.

Peach & Strawberry Tart

SERVES: 4

PREP: 20 MINS +
1 HR 15 MINS
REST/COOL

COOKING: 15 MINS

Ingredients

PASTRY

*200 g/7 oz plain flour, plus extra
for dusting*

*100 g/3½ oz butter, diced, plus
extra for greasing*

50 g/1¾ oz icing sugar, sifted

finely grated rind of 1 orange

1 egg yolk, beaten

3 tbsp milk

FILLING

175 ml/6 fl oz double cream

4 tbsp icing sugar

1 tbsp peach liqueur

4 tbsp strawberry jam

2 peaches, stoned and sliced

*100 g/3½ oz strawberries, hulled
and sliced*

icing sugar, to dust

whipped cream, to serve

To make the pastry, sift the flour into a bowl. Rub in the butter, then mix in the icing sugar, orange rind, egg yolk and milk. Knead briefly on a lightly floured work surface, then leave to rest for 30 minutes. Preheat the oven to 180°C/350°F/Gas Mark 4. Grease a 23-cm/9-inch flan tin with butter. Roll out the pastry to a thickness of 5 mm/¼ inch and use to line the base and sides of the tin. Prick all over the base with a fork, line with baking paper and fill with baking beans. Bake for 15 minutes. Remove from the oven and reserve.

To make the filling, put the cream into a bowl and beat in the icing sugar. Stir in the peach liqueur. Spread the bottom of the pastry shell with strawberry jam, then spoon in the cream filling. Arrange the sliced peaches and strawberries over the top, then cover with clingfilm and refrigerate for 45 minutes. Remove from the refrigerator, dust with icing sugar and serve with whipped cream.

Blueberry Clafoutis

SERVES: 4

PREP: 15 MINS

COOKING: 30 MINS

Ingredients

2 tbsp butter, plus extra
  for greasing
125 g/4½ oz caster sugar
3 eggs
60 g/2¼ oz plain flour, sifted
250 ml/9 fl oz single cream
½ tsp ground cinnamon
450 g/1 lb blueberries

icing sugar, to dust

single cream, to serve

Preheat the oven to 180°C/350°F/Gas Mark 4. Grease a 1-litre/1¾-pint ovenproof dish with butter.

Put the remaining butter into a bowl with the sugar, and cream together until fluffy. Add the eggs and beat together well. Mix in the flour, then gradually stir in the cream followed by the cinnamon. Continue to stir until smooth.

Arrange the blueberries in the bottom of the prepared dish, then pour over the cream batter. Transfer to the preheated oven and bake for about 30 minutes, or until puffed and golden. Remove from the oven, dust with icing sugar and serve with single cream.

SERVES: 4

PREP: 20 MINS +
30 MINS
RESTING

COOKING: 45 MINS

Forest Fruit Pie

Ingredients

250 g/9 oz blueberries

250 g/9 oz raspberries

250 g/9 oz blackberries

100 g/3½ oz caster sugar

200 g/7 oz plain flour, plus extra
for dusting

25 g/1 oz ground hazelnuts

100 g/3½ oz butter, diced, plus
extra for greasing

finely grated rind of 1 lemon

1 egg yolk, beaten

4 tbsp milk

2 tsp icing sugar, to dust

whipped cream, to serve

Put the fruit into a saucepan with 3 tablespoons of caster sugar and simmer, stirring, for 5 minutes. Remove from the heat. Sift the flour into a bowl, then add the hazelnuts. Rub in the butter, then sift in the remaining sugar. Add the lemon rind, egg yolk and 3 tablespoons of milk and mix. Turn out onto a lightly floured work surface and knead briefly. Leave to rest for 30 minutes.

Preheat the oven to 190°C/375°F/Gas Mark 5. Grease a 20-cm/8-inch ovenproof pie dish with butter. Roll out half the pastry to a thickness of 5 mm/¼ inch and use it to line the dish. Spoon the fruit into the pastry shell. Brush the rim with water, then roll out the remaining dough and use it to cover the pie. Trim and crimp round the edges, make 2 small slits in the top and decorate with 2 leaf shapes cut from the dough trimmings. Brush all over with the remaining milk. Bake for 40 minutes. Remove from the oven, sprinkle over the icing sugar and serve with whipped cream.

Banoffee Pie

SERVES: 4

PREP: 20 MINS +
1 HR COOLING

COOKING: 2 HRS 15 MINS

Ingredients

two 400 ml/14 fl oz cans sweetened
condensed milk

6 tbsp butter, melted

150 g/5½ oz digestive biscuits,
crushed into crumbs

50 g/1¾ oz almonds, toasted
and ground

50 g/1¾ oz hazelnuts, toasted
and ground

4 ripe bananas

1 tbsp lemon juice

1 tsp vanilla essence

75 g/2¾ oz chocolate, grated

450 ml/16 fl oz thick double
cream, whipped

Place the cans of milk in a large saucepan and cover them with water. Bring to the boil, then reduce the heat and simmer for 2 hours. Ensure the water is topped up regularly to keep the cans covered. Carefully lift out the hot cans and leave to cool.

Preheat the oven to 180°C/350°F/Gas Mark 4. Grease a 23-cm/9-inch flan tin with butter. Put the remaining butter into a bowl and add the biscuits and nuts. Mix together well, then press the mixture evenly into the base and sides of the flan tin. Bake for 10-12 minutes, then remove from the oven and leave to cool.

Peel and slice the bananas and put them into a bowl. Sprinkle over the lemon juice and vanilla essence and mix gently. Spread the banana mixture over the biscuit crust in the tin, then open the cans of condensed milk and spoon the contents over the bananas. Sprinkle over 50 g/1¾ oz of the chocolate, then top with a thick layer of whipped cream. Scatter over the remaining chocolate and serve.

65

Manhattan Cheesecake

SERVES: 8-10

PREP: 20 MINS +
10 HRS
COOLING/
CHILLING

COOKING: 35 MINS

Ingredients

sunflower oil, for brushing

85 g/3 oz butter

*200 g/7 oz digestive biscuits,
  crushed*

400 g/14 oz cream cheese

2 large eggs

140 g/5 oz caster sugar

1½ tsp vanilla essence

450 ml/16 fl oz soured cream

BLUEBERRY TOPPING

55 g/2 oz caster sugar

4 tbsp water

250 g/9 oz fresh blueberries

1 tsp arrowroot

Preheat the oven to 190°C/375°F/Gas Mark 5. Brush a 20-cm/8-inch springform tin with oil. Melt the butter in a saucepan over a low heat. Stir in the biscuits, then spread in the tin. Place the cream cheese, eggs, 100 g/3½ oz of the sugar and ½ teaspoon of the vanilla essence in a food processor. Process until smooth. Pour over the biscuit base and smooth the top. Place on a baking tray and bake for 20 minutes, or until set. Remove from the oven and leave to stand for 20 minutes. Leave the oven switched on.

Mix the cream with the remaining sugar and vanilla essence in a bowl. Spoon over the cheesecake. Return it to the oven for 10 minutes, leave to cool, then chill in the refrigerator for 8 hours or overnight.

To make the topping, place the sugar in a saucepan with half of the water over a low heat and stir until the sugar has dissolved. Increase the heat, add the blueberries, cover and cook for a few minutes, or until they begin to soften. Remove from the heat. Mix the arrowroot and remaining water in a bowl, add to the fruit and stir until smooth. Return to a low heat. Cook until the juice thickens and turns translucent. Leave to cool. Remove the cheesecake from the tin 1 hour before serving. Spoon the fruit on top and chill until ready to serve.

67

Strawberry Roulade

SERVES: 8

PREP: 30 MINS

COOKING: 10 MINS

Ingredients

3 large eggs

125 g/4½ oz caster sugar

125 g/4½ oz plain flour

1 tbsp hot water

FILLING

200 ml/7 fl oz low-fat fromage frais

1 tsp almond essence

225 g/8 oz small strawberries

TO DECORATE

1 tbsp flaked almonds, toasted

1 tsp icing sugar

Line a 35 x 25-cm/14 x 10-inch Swiss roll tin with baking paper. Place the eggs in a mixing bowl with the caster sugar. Place the bowl over a pan of hot, but not boiling water and whisk until pale and thick.

Remove the bowl from the pan. Sieve in the flour and fold into the eggs with the hot water. Pour the mixture into the tin and bake in a preheated oven, 220°C/425°F/Gas Mark 7, for about 8-10 minutes, until golden and set.

Transfer the mixture to a sheet of baking paper. Peel off the lining paper and roll up the sponge tightly along with the baking paper. Wrap in a tea towel and set aside to cool.

Mix together the fromage frais and the almond essence. Reserving a few strawberries for decoration, wash, hull and slice the remainder. Leave the fromage frais mixture and strawberries to chill in the refrigerator until required.

Unroll the sponge, spread the fromage frais mixture over the sponge and sprinkle with the sliced strawberries. Roll the sponge up again and transfer to a serving plate. Sprinkle with almonds and lightly dust with icing sugar. Decorate with the reserved strawberries.

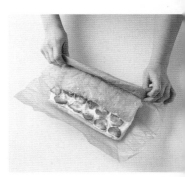

Raspberry Dessert Cake

Ingredients

225 g/8 oz butter, plus extra
for greasing

250 g/9 oz plain chocolate,
broken into pieces

1 tbsp strong dark coffee

5 eggs

85 g/3 oz golden caster sugar

85 g/3 oz plain flour

1 tsp ground cinnamon

175 g/6 oz fresh raspberries

icing sugar, for dusting

TO SERVE

fresh raspberries
whipped cream

Preheat the oven to 160°C/325°F/Gas Mark 3.
Grease a 23-cm/9-inch cake tin with butter and line
the base with baking paper. Place the chocolate, butter
and coffee in a small heatproof bowl and set over a
saucepan of gently simmering water until melted.
Stir, then remove from the heat and cool slightly.

Place the eggs and sugar in a separate bowl and beat
together until thick and pale. Gently fold in the
chocolate mixture. Sift the flour and ground cinnamon
into a separate bowl, then fold into the chocolate
mixture. Pour into the prepared tin and sprinkle the
raspberries evenly over the top.

Bake in the hot oven for 35-45 minutes, or until the
cake is well risen and springy to the touch. Leave to
cool in the tin for 15 minutes before turning out on to a
large serving plate. Dust with icing sugar before
serving with fresh raspberries and cream.

Chocolate Panforte

SERVES: 4-6

PREP: 20 MINS +
           1 HR COOLING

COOKING: 1 HR

Ingredients

100 g/3½ oz candied orange peel

50 g/1¾ oz dried apricots, chopped

2 tbsp orange-flavoured liqueur,
  such as Cointreau

100 g/3½ oz shelled whole hazelnuts

150 g/5½ oz split almonds, toasted

100 g/3½ oz plain flour

2 tbsp unsweetened cocoa powder

2 tsp mixed spice

125 g/4½ oz caster sugar

150 ml/5 fl oz clear honey

icing sugar, to decorate

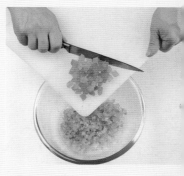

Preheat the oven to 150°C/300°F/Gas Mark 2. Line a 20-cm/8-inch round cake tin.

Put the orange peel, apricots and liqueur into a heatproof bowl and leave to soak. Toast the hazelnuts under a preheated medium grill until the skins split, remove to a clean tea towel and rub to remove the skins. Coarsely chop, then add to the fruit with the almonds and mix well. Sift the flour, cocoa powder and mixed spice into a separate bowl, then mix into the fruit and nuts. Bring the sugar and honey to the boil in a saucepan over a low heat, stirring. Continue to boil, stirring, for 5 minutes, then quickly pour the syrup over the fruit and mix well. Turn into the prepared tin and level the surface. Bake in the oven for 50 minutes.

Remove from the oven, turn out on to a wire rack and discard the lining paper. Leave to cool, then dredge with icing sugar. Serve immediately or store for up to 3-4 months in an airtight container.

Crème Brûlée Tarts

SERVES: 6

PREP: *16 HRS 20 MINS*

COOKING: *25 MINS*

Ingredients

PASTRY

150 g/5½ oz plain flour

25 g/1 oz caster sugar

*125 g/4½ oz butter, cut into
  small pieces*

1 tbsp water

FILLING

4 egg yolks

50 g/1¾ oz caster sugar

400 ml/14 fl oz double cream

1 tsp vanilla essence

demerara sugar, for sprinkling

To make the pastry, place the flour and sugar in a bowl and rub in the butter with your fingertips until the mixture resembles breadcrumbs. Add the water and work the mixture together until a soft dough has formed. Wrap in clingfilm and chill for 30 minutes.

Divide the dough into 6 pieces. Roll out each piece on a lightly floured surface to line 6 tart tins 10 cm/ 4 inches wide. Prick the bottom of the pastry with a fork and chill for 20 minutes.

Line the pastry cases with foil and baking beans and bake in a preheated oven, 190°C/375°F/Gas Mark 5, for 15 minutes. Remove the foil and beans and cook the pastry cases for a further 10 minutes until crisp. Leave to cool.

Meanwhile, make the filling. In a bowl, beat the egg yolks and sugar until pale. Heat the cream and vanilla essence in a pan until just below boiling point, then pour it on to the egg mixture, whisking constantly.

Return the mixture to a clean pan and bring to just below the boil, stirring, until thick. Do not allow the mixture to boil or it will curdle.

Leave the mixture to cool slightly, then pour it into the tart tins. Leave to cool and then chill overnight.

Sprinkle the tarts with the sugar. Place under a preheated hot grill for a few minutes. Leave to cool, then chill for 2 hours before serving.

Chocolate Fudge Cake

Ingredients

175 g/6 oz unsalted butter,
  softened, plus extra for greasing

175 g/6 oz golden caster sugar

3 eggs, beaten

3 tbsp golden syrup

40 g/1½ oz ground almonds

175 g/6 oz self-raising flour

pinch of salt

40 g/1½ oz cocoa powder

ICING

225 g/8 oz plain chocolate,
  broken into pieces

55 g/2 oz dark muscovado sugar

225 g/8 oz unsalted butter, diced

5 tbsp evaporated milk

½ tsp vanilla essence

Grease and line the base of 2 x 20-cm/8-inch cake tins. To make the icing, place the chocolate, sugar, butter, evaporated milk and vanilla essence in a heavy-based saucepan. Heat gently, stirring constantly, until melted. Pour into a bowl and leave to cool. Cover and chill in the refrigerator for 1 hour, or until spreadable.

Preheat the oven to 180°C/350°F/Gas Mark 4. Place the butter and sugar in a bowl and beat together until light and fluffy. Gradually beat in the eggs. Stir in the syrup and ground almonds. Sift the flour, salt and cocoa powder into a separate bowl, then fold into the mixture. Add a little water, if necessary, to make a dropping consistency. Spoon the mixture into the prepared tins and bake in the oven for 30-35 minutes, or until springy to the touch and a skewer inserted in the centre comes out clean.

Leave the cakes in the tins for 5 minutes, then turn out on to wire racks to cool completely. When the cakes are cold, sandwich them together with half the icing. Spread the remaining icing over the top and sides of the cake, swirling it to give a frosted appearance.

SERVES: 8

PREP: 25 MINS +
            2 HRS
            COOLING/
            CHILLING

COOKING: 35-45 MINS

SERVES: 8

PREP: 10 MINS

COOKING: 10 MINS

Cherry Scones

Ingredients

6 tbsp butter, cut into small pieces,
plus extra for greasing

225 g/8 oz self-raising flour

15 g/½ oz caster sugar

pinch of salt

40 g/1½ oz glacé cherries, chopped

40 g/1½ oz sultanas

1 egg, beaten

50 ml/2 fl oz milk

plain flour, for dusting

Preheat the oven to 220°C/425°F/Gas Mark 7. Lightly grease a baking tray with a little butter. Sift the flour, sugar and salt into a large bowl. Add the butter and rub in with your fingertips until the mixture resembles breadcrumbs. Stir in the glacé cherries and sultanas. Add the egg. Reserve 1 tablespoon of the milk for glazing, then add the remainder to the mixture. Mix together to form a soft dough.

On a lightly floured work surface, roll out the dough to a thickness of 2 cm/¾ inch and cut out 8 scones, using a 5-cm/2-inch cutter. Place the scones on the baking tray and brush the tops with the reserved milk.

Bake in the preheated oven for 8-10 minutes, or until the scones are golden brown. Leave to cool on a wire rack, then serve split and buttered, if you like.

Chelsea Buns

Ingredients

25 g/1 oz butter, plus extra
for greasing

225 g/8 oz strong white bread flour,
plus extra for dusting

½ tsp salt

2 tsp easy-blend dried yeast

1 tsp golden caster sugar

125 ml/4 fl oz tepid milk

1 egg, beaten

vegetable oil, for brushing

85 g/3 oz icing sugar, to glaze

FILLING

55 g/2 oz light muscovado sugar

115 g/4 oz luxury mixed dried fruits

1 tsp ground mixed spice

55 g/2 oz butter, softened

Grease an 18-cm/7-inch square cake tin. Sift the flour and salt into a warmed bowl, stir in the yeast and sugar and rub in the butter. Make a well in the centre. In a separate bowl, mix the milk and egg and pour into the dry ingredients. Beat to make a soft dough. Turn out on to a floured work surface and knead for 5-10 minutes, or until smooth. Brush a clean bowl with oil, place the dough in the bowl, cover with clingfilm and leave in a warm place for 1 hour, or until doubled in size.

Turn the dough out on to a floured surface and knead lightly for 1 minute. Roll out into a 30 x 23-cm/12 x 9-inch rectangle.

To make the filling, place the muscovado sugar, fruit and spice in a bowl and mix. Spread the dough with the softened butter and sprinkle the fruit mixture on top. Roll up from a long side, then cut into 9 pieces. Place in the prepared tin, cut-side up. Cover with oiled clingfilm and leave in a warm place for 45 minutes, or until well risen.

Preheat the oven to 190°C/375°F/Gas Mark 5. Bake the buns in the oven for 30 minutes, or until golden. Leave to cool in the tin for 10 minutes, then transfer, in one piece, to a wire rack to cool. Sift the icing sugar into a bowl and stir in enough water to make a thin glaze. Brush over the buns and leave to set. Pull the buns apart to serve.

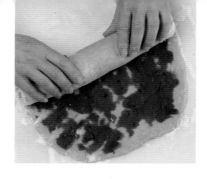

Simple Cinnamon Rolls

Ingredients

350 g/12 oz self-raising flour

  pinch of salt

2 tbsp caster sugar

1 tsp ground cinnamon

100 g/3½ oz butter, melted, plus
  extra for greasing

2 egg yolks

200 ml/7 fl oz milk, plus extra
  for glazing

FILLING

1 tsp ground cinnamon

55 g/2 oz soft brown sugar

2 tbsp caster sugar

1 tbsp butter, melted

ICING

125 g/4½ oz icing sugar, sifted

2 tbsp cream cheese, softened

1 tbsp butter, softened

about 30 ml/1 fl oz boiling water

1 tsp vanilla essence

Preheat the oven to 180°C/350°F/Gas Mark 4. Grease a 20-cm/8-inch round tin and line the base with baking paper.

Mix the flour, salt, caster sugar and cinnamon together in a large bowl. Whisk the butter, egg yolks and milk together and combine with the dry ingredients to make a soft dough. Turn out on to a large piece of greaseproof paper, lightly sprinkled with flour, and roll out to a rectangle 30 x 25 cm/ 12 x 10 inches.

To make the filling, mix the ingredients together, spread evenly over the dough and roll up, Swiss-roll style, to form a log. Using a sharp knife, cut the dough into 8 even-sized slices and pack into the prepared tin. Brush gently with extra milk and bake for 30-35 minutes, or until golden brown. Remove from the oven and leave to cool for 5 minutes before removing from the tin.

Sift the icing sugar into a large bowl and make a well in the centre. Place the cream cheese and butter in the centre, pour over the water and stir to mix. Add extra boiling water, a few drops at a time, until the icing coats the back of a spoon. Stir in the vanilla essence. Drizzle over the rolls. Serve warm or cold.

Apple Shortcakes

MAKES: 4

PREP: 25 MINS

COOKING: 25 MINS

Ingredients

2 tbsp butter, cut into small pieces, plus extra for greasing

150 g/5½ oz plain flour, plus extra for dusting

½ tsp salt

1 tsp baking powder

1 tbsp caster sugar

50 ml/2 fl oz milk

icing sugar, for dusting (optional)

FILLING

3 dessert apples, peeled, cored and sliced

100 g/3½ oz caster sugar

1 tbsp lemon juice

1 tsp ground cinnamon

300 ml/10 fl oz water

150 ml/5 fl oz double cream, lightly whipped

Preheat the oven to 220°C/425°F/Gas Mark 7. Lightly grease a baking tray. Sift the flour, salt and baking powder into a large bowl. Stir in the sugar, then add the butter and rub in with your fingertips until the mixture resembles fine breadcrumbs. Pour in the milk and mix to a soft dough.

On a lightly floured work surface, knead the dough lightly, then roll out to 1-cm/½-inch thick. Stamp out 4 rounds, using a 5-cm/2-inch cutter. Transfer the rounds to the prepared baking tray.

Bake in the oven for 15 minutes, until the shortcakes are well risen and lightly browned. Leave to cool.

To make the filling, place the apple, sugar, lemon juice and cinnamon in a saucepan. Add the water, bring to the boil and simmer, uncovered, for 5-10 minutes, until the apples are tender. Cool slightly, then remove the apples from the saucepan.

To serve, split the shortcakes in half. Place each bottom half on an individual serving plate and spoon on a quarter of the apple slices, then the cream. Place the other half of the shortcake on top. Serve dusted with icing sugar, if wished.

Apricot Slices

Ingredients

PASTRY

100 g/3½ oz vegan margarine, cut into small pieces, plus extra for greasing

225 g/8 oz wholemeal flour

50 g/1¾ oz finely ground mixed nuts

4 tbsp water

soya milk, to glaze

FILLING

225 g/8 oz dried apricots

grated rind of 1 orange

300 ml/10 fl oz apple juice

1 tsp ground cinnamon

50 g/1¾ oz raisins

Lightly grease a 23-cm/9-inch square cake tin. To make the pastry, place the flour and nuts in a mixing bowl and rub in the margarine with your fingers until the mixture resembles breadcrumbs. Stir in the water and bring together to form a dough. Wrap and set aside to chill in the refrigerator for 30 minutes.

To make the filling, place the apricots, orange rind and apple juice in a pan and bring to the boil. Simmer for 30 minutes, until the apricots are mushy. Cool slightly, then process in a food processor or blender to a purée. Alternatively, press the mixture through a sieve. Stir in the cinnamon and raisins.

Divide the pastry in half, roll out one half and use to line the base of the tin. Spread the apricot purée over the top and brush the edges of the pastry with water. Roll out the rest of the dough to fit over the top of the apricot purée. Press down and seal the edges.

Prick the top of the pastry with a fork and brush with soya milk. Bake in a preheated oven, 200°C/400°F/ Gas Mark 6, for 20-25 minutes until the pastry is golden. Leave to cool slightly before cutting into 12 bars. Serve either warm or cold.

MAKES: 8

PREP: 10 MINS +
         30 MINS
         COOLING

COOKING: 15 MINS

Shortbread Fantails

Ingredients

125 g/4½ oz butter, softened,
  plus extra for greasing

40 g/1½ oz granulated sugar

25 g/1 oz icing sugar

225 g/8 oz plain flour, plus extra
  for dusting

salt

2 tsp orange flower water

caster sugar, for sprinkling

Preheat the oven to 150°C/300°F/Gas Mark 2, then lightly grease a 20-cm/8-inch shallow round cake tin. Beat the butter, granulated sugar and icing sugar together in a large bowl until light and fluffy. Sift the flour and a pinch of salt into the mixture, then add the orange flower water. Mix together to form a soft dough.

Roll out the dough on a lightly floured work surface, to a 20-cm/8-inch round and place in the prepared tin. Prick the dough well and score into 8 triangles with a round-bladed knife.

Bake in the preheated oven for 30-35 minutes, or until the shortbread is crisp and a pale golden colour.

Sprinkle with caster sugar, then cut along the marked lines to make the 8 fantails. Leave the shortbread to cool before removing the pieces from the tin. Store in an airtight container for several days.

Caramel Chocolate Shortbread

MAKES:	24
PREP:	10 MINS + 1 HR CHILLING/ SETTING
COOKING:	30 MINS

Ingredients

115 g/4 oz butter, plus extra
  for greasing

175 g/6 oz plain flour

55 g/2 oz golden caster sugar

FILLING AND TOPPING

175 g/6 oz butter

115 g/4 oz golden caster sugar

3 tbsp golden syrup

400 g/14 oz canned condensed milk

200 g/7 oz plain chocolate,
  broken into pieces

Preheat the oven to 180°C/350°F/Gas Mark 4.
Grease and line the base of a 23-cm/9-inch shallow
square cake tin. Place the butter, flour and sugar in a
food processor and process until it begins to bind
together. Press the mixture into the tin and smooth the
top. Bake in the preheated oven, for 20-25 minutes, or
until golden.

Meanwhile, make the filling. Place the butter, sugar,
syrup and condensed milk in a saucepan and heat
gently until the sugar has melted. Bring to the boil and
simmer for 6-8 minutes, stirring constantly, until the
mixture becomes very thick. Pour over the shortbread
base and leave to chill in the refrigerator until firm.

To make the topping, melt the chocolate and leave to
cool, then spread over the caramel. Chill in the
refrigerator until set. Cut the shortbread into 12 pieces
with a sharp knife and serve.

Lemon Drops

Ingredients

115 g/4 oz butter or margarine,
  plus extra for greasing

200 g/7 oz caster sugar

2 tbsp lemon juice

1 tbsp finely grated lemon rind

2 tbsp water

225 g/8 oz plain flour, sifted

1 tsp bicarbonate of soda

½ tsp cream of tartar

TO DECORATE

icing sugar

crystallised fruit, chopped finely
  (optional)

Preheat the oven to 180°C/350°F/Gas Mark 4. Grease a large baking sheet. Beat together the butter, caster sugar, lemon juice, lemon rind and water.

In a separate bowl, mix together the flour, bicarbonate of soda and cream of tartar. Add the butter mixture and blend together well.

Spoon the mixture into a piping bag fitted with a star-shaped nozzle. Pipe 24 fancy drops, about the size of a tablespoon, on to the greased baking sheet, allowing room for the biscuits to spread during cooking. Transfer to the preheated oven and bake for 10 minutes, or until the lemon drops are golden brown.

Remove from the oven, then transfer to a wire rack and leave to cool completely. Dust with icing sugar and sprinkle over the crystallized fruit, if liked.

Lemon Jumbles

MAKES: 50
PREP: 10 MINS
COOKING: 20 MINS

Ingredients

100 g/3½ oz butter, softened, plus extra for greasing

125 g/4½ oz caster sugar

grated rind of 1 lemon

1 egg, beaten

4 tbsp lemon juice

350 g/12 oz plain flour

1 tsp baking powder

1 tbsp milk

icing sugar, for dredging

Lightly grease several baking trays with a little butter.

In a mixing bowl, cream together the butter, caster sugar and lemon rind until pale and fluffy.

Add the beaten egg and lemon juice, a little at a time, beating well after each addition.

Sieve the flour and baking powder into the creamed mixture and blend together. Add the milk, mixing to form a soft dough.

Turn the dough out on to a lightly floured work surface and divide into about 50 equal-size pieces.

Roll each piece into a sausage shape with your hands and twist in the middle to make an 'S' shape.

Place on the prepared baking trays and bake in a preheated oven, 170°C/325°F/Gas Mark 3, for 15-20 minutes. Carefully transfer to a wire rack and set aside to cool completely. Dredge with icing sugar to serve.

Chocolate Viennese Fingers

MAKES: 30

PREP: 20 MINS +
40 MINS
COOLING/
SETTING

COOKING: 15 MINS

Ingredients

115 g/4 oz butter, softened, plus
  extra for greasing

55 g/2 oz golden icing sugar, sifted

125 g/4½ oz plain flour

1 tbsp cocoa powder

100 g/3½ oz plain chocolate,
  melted and cooled

Preheat the oven to 180°C/350°F/Gas Mark 4.
Grease 2 baking sheets. Beat the butter and sugar
together until light and fluffy. Sift the flour and cocoa
powder into the bowl and work the mixture until it is
a smooth, piping consistency.

Spoon into a large piping bag fitted with a 2.5-cm/
1-inch fluted nozzle. Pipe 6-cm/2½-inch lengths of
the mixture on to the prepared baking sheets,
allowing room for expansion during cooking. Bake in
the preheated oven for 15 minutes, or until firm.

Leave to cool on the baking sheets for 2 minutes, then
transfer to a wire rack to cool completely. Dip the
ends of the biscuits into the melted chocolate and
leave to set before serving.

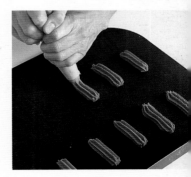

MAKES:	30
PREP:	12 MINS
COOKING:	12 MINS

Chewy Golden Cookies

Ingredients

*175 g/6 oz butter or margarine,
 plus extra for greasing*

275 g/9½ oz light muscovado sugar

225 ml/8 fl oz golden syrup

3 egg whites

500 g/1 lb 2 oz rolled oats

280 g/10 oz plain flour

pinch of salt

1 tsp baking powder

icing sugar, to drizzle

Preheat the oven to 180°C/350°F/Gas Mark 4 and grease a large baking sheet.

In a large mixing bowl, blend the butter (or margarine, if using), sugar, syrup and egg whites together. Gradually add the oats, flour, salt and baking powder and mix thoroughly.

Drop 30 rounded tablespoonfuls of the mixture onto the baking sheet and transfer to the preheated oven.

Bake for 12 minutes, or until the cookies are light brown.

Remove from the oven and let them cool on a wire rack. Drizzle over the icing sugar and serve.

Nutty Chocolate Drizzles

MAKES: 24

PREP: 10 MINS

COOKING: 12 MINS

Ingredients

225 g/8 oz butter or margarine,
    plus extra for greasing

275 g/9½ oz demerara sugar

1 egg

140g/5 oz plain flour, sifted

1 tsp baking powder

1 tsp bicarbonate of soda

125 g/4½ oz rolled oats

20 g/¾ oz bran

20 g/¾ oz wheatgerm

115 g/4 oz mixed nuts, toasted
    and chopped roughly

90 g/3¼ oz plain chocolate chips

115 g/4 oz raisins and sultanas

175 g/6 oz plain chocolate,
    chopped roughly

Preheat the oven to 180°C/350°F/Gas Mark 4. Grease a large baking sheet. In a large bowl, cream together the butter, sugar and egg. Add the flour, baking powder, bicarbonate of soda, oats, bran and wheatgerm and mix together until well combined. Stir in the nuts, chocoate chips and dried fruit.

Put 24 rounded tablespoonfuls of the cookie mixture onto the greased baking sheet. Transfer to the preheated oven and bake for 12 minutes, or until the cookies are golden brown.

Remove the cookies from the oven, transfer to a wire rack and let them cool. While they are cooling, put the chocolate pieces into a heatproof bowl over a pan of gently simmering water and heat until melted. Stir the chocolate, then allow to cool slightly. Use a spoon to drizzle the chocolate in waves over the cookies, or spoon it into a piping nozzle and pipe zigzag lines over the cookies. Store in an airtight container in the refrigerator before serving.

Savoury Bites

Of course the pleasures of home baking are not all about

sweet things and this chapter is brimming with tasty savoury ideas for

party nibbles, lunchtime snacks, picnic treats and after-school fillers.

Cheese is top of the list for flavourings, whether classic

Cheese Straws (see page 114) to serve with pre-dinner drinks or the less

familiar but no less delightful Cheese & Mustard Scones (see page 105)

for a weekend brunch table. However, don't worry if cheese is not your

favourite as there are lots of other fabulous flavours, such as spicy

Savoury Curried Biscuits (see page 112), aromatic Pesto Palmiers

(see page 117) and superb Bacon & Polenta Muffins (see page 106).

There are also recipes for timeless treats. There can be no better way to

start the morning than with Fresh Croissants (see page 96) and no better

way to end the afternoon than with Teacakes (see page 98).

Fresh Croissants

MAKES: 12

PREP: 12 HRS

COOKING: 15-20 MINS

Ingredients

500 g/1 lb 2 oz strong white bread flour, plus extra for rolling

40 g/1½ oz caster sugar

1 tsp salt

2 tsp easy-blend dried yeast

300 ml/10 fl oz milk, heated until just warm to the touch

300 g/10½ oz butter, softened, plus extra for greasing

1 egg, lightly beaten with 1 tbsp milk, for glazing

Preheat the oven to 200°C/400°F/Gas Mark 6. Stir the dry ingredients into a large bowl, make a well in the centre and add the milk. Mix to a soft dough, adding more milk if too dry. Knead on a lightly floured work surface for 5-10 minutes, or until smooth and elastic. Leave to rise in a large greased bowl, covered, in a warm place until doubled in size. Meanwhile, flatten the butter with a rolling pin between 2 sheets of greaseproof paper to form a rectangle about 5 mm/¼ inch thick, then chill.

Knead the dough for 1 minute. Remove the butter from the refrigerator and leave to soften slightly. Roll out the dough on a well-floured work surface to 46 x 15 cm/18 x 6 inches. Place the butter in the centre, folding up the sides and squeezing the edges together gently. With the short end of the dough towards you, fold the top third down towards the centre, then fold the bottom third up. Rotate 90° clockwise so that the fold is to your left and the top flap towards your right. Roll out to a rectangle and fold again. If the butter feels soft, wrap the dough in clingfilm and chill. Repeat the rolling process twice more. Cut the dough in half. Roll out one half into a triangle 5 mm/¼ inch thick (keep the other half refrigerated). Use a cardboard triangular template, base 18 cm/7 inches and sides 20 cm/8 inches, to cut out the croissants.

Brush the triangles lightly with the glaze. Roll into croissant shapes, starting at the base and tucking the point underneath to prevent unrolling while cooking. Brush again with the glaze. Place on an ungreased baking tray and leave to double in size. Bake for 15-20 minutes until golden brown.

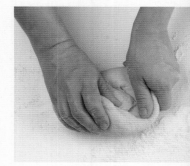

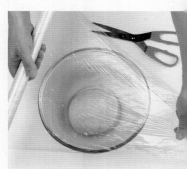

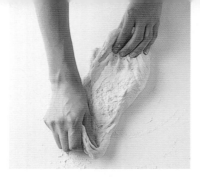

Teacakes

SERVES: 12

PREP: 30 MINS +
3 HRS
RISING/
COOLING

COOKING: 20 MINS

Ingredients

*2 tbsp butter, cut into small pieces,
plus extra for greasing*

*450 g/1 lb strong white bread flour,
plus extra for dusting*

1 sachet easy-blend dried yeast

50 g/1¾ oz caster sugar

1 tsp salt

300 ml/10 fl oz hand-hot milk

75 g/2¾ oz luxury dried fruit mix

honey, for brushing

butter, to serve

Grease several baking trays with a little butter.
Sift the flour into a large bowl. Stir in the dried yeast,
sugar and salt. Add the butter and rub in with your
fingertips until the mixture resembles fine
breadcrumbs. Add the milk and mix together to form
a soft dough.

Place the dough on a lightly floured work surface and
knead for 5 minutes. Alternatively, knead the dough
with an electric mixer with a dough hook. Place the
dough in a greased bowl, cover and leave to rise in a
warm place for 1-1½ hours, or until doubled in size.

Knead the dough again for a few minutes, then knead
in the fruit. Divide the dough into 12 rounds and place
on the baking trays. Cover and leave for 1 further
hour, or until springy to the touch.

Preheat the oven to 200°C/400°F/Gas Mark 6, then
bake the teacakes for 20 minutes. Brush with honey
while still warm, then transfer the teacakes to
a wire rack to cool completely before serving them
split in half and toasted, if wished. Spread with butter
and serve.

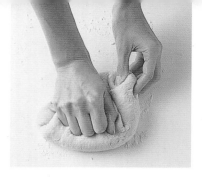

Sun-dried Tomato Rolls

Ingredients

100 g/3½ oz butter, melted and cooled slightly, plus extra for greasing

225 g/8 oz strong white bread flour, plus extra for dusting

½ tsp salt

1 sachet easy-blend dried yeast

3 tbsp milk, warmed

2 eggs, beaten

50 g/1¾ oz sun-dried tomatoes in oil, drained and finely chopped

milk, for brushing

Lightly grease a baking tray with a little butter.

Sieve the flour and salt into a large mixing bowl. Stir in the yeast, then pour in the melted butter, milk and beaten eggs. Bring together with your fingers to form a dough.

Turn the dough out on to a lightly floured work surface and knead for about 5 minutes, until smooth. Alternatively, use an electric mixer with a dough hook.

Place the dough in a greased bowl, cover and leave to rise in a warm place for 1-1½ hours, or until it has doubled in size.

Knead the dough for 2-3 minutes to knock it back, then knead in the sun-dried tomatoes, sprinkling the work surface with a little extra flour because the tomatoes are quite oily.

Divide the dough into 8 even-sized balls and place them on the prepared baking tray. Cover and leave to rise for about 30 minutes, or until the rolls have doubled in size.

Brush the rolls with milk and bake in a preheated oven, 230°C/450°F/Gas Mark 8, for 10-15 minutes, or until they are golden brown.

Transfer the tomato rolls to a wire rack and leave to cool slightly before serving.

Cheesy Bread

Ingredients

2 tbsp butter, melted, plus extra
  for greasing

225 g/8 oz self-raising flour

1 tsp salt

1 tsp mustard powder

100 g/3½ oz mature cheese, grated

2 tbsp snipped fresh chives

1 egg, beaten

150 ml/5 fl oz milk

Preheat the oven to 190°C/375°F/Gas Mark 5.
Grease a 23-cm/9-inch square cake tin with a little
butter and line the base with baking paper.

Sift the flour, salt and mustard powder into a large
bowl. Reserve 3 tablespoons of the grated mature
cheese for sprinkling, then stir the remaining grated
cheese into the bowl, together with the snipped
chives. Mix together well. Add the beaten egg, melted
butter and milk to the dry ingredients and stir
thoroughly to combine.

Pour the mixture into the tin and spread with a knife.
Sprinkle over the reserved grated cheese.

Bake in the preheated oven for 30 minutes. Leave the
bread to cool slightly in the tin. Turn out on to a wire
rack to cool completely. Cut into triangles to serve.

SERVES: 8

PREP: 25 MINS +
        30 MINS
        COOLING

COOKING: 30 MINS

Cheese & Chive Scones

Ingredients

40 g/1½ oz butter, plus extra
   for greasing

115 g/4 oz white self-raising flour,
   plus extra for dusting

115 g/4 oz wholemeal self-raising
   flour

1 tsp baking powder

pinch of salt

85 g/3 oz finely grated Cheddar
   cheese

2 tbsp snipped fresh chives

3 tbsp milk

fresh chives, to garnish

Preheat the oven to 220°C/425°F/Gas Mark 7,
then grease a baking sheet. Sift the 2 flours, baking
powder and salt into a bowl. Rub in the butter until the
mixture resembles fine breadcrumbs, then stir in
55 g/2 oz of the grated cheese and chives. Stir in up to
1 tablespoon of milk to make a fairly soft, light dough.

On a floured work surface, roll out the dough to
2 cm/¾ inch thick and stamp into rounds with a
6-cm/2½-inch plain cutter. Gather the trimmings,
re-roll and stamp out more scones until the dough is
used up.

Place the scones on the prepared baking sheet, brush
the tops with the remaining milk and sprinkle with the
remaining grated cheese. Bake in the preheated oven
for 10 minutes, or until well risen and golden. Garnish
with fresh chives and serve warm or cold.

Cheese & Mustard Scones

MAKES: 8

PREP: 15 MINS

COOKING: 15 MINS

Ingredients

4 tbsp butter, diced, plus extra
for greasing

225 g/8 oz self-raising flour, plus
extra for dusting

1 tsp baking powder

125 g/4½ oz mature cheese, grated

1 tsp mustard powder

150 ml/5 fl oz milk, plus extra
for brushing

salt and pepper

Lightly grease a baking tray with a little butter.

Sieve the flour, baking powder and a pinch of salt into a bowl. Rub in the butter with your fingers until the mixture resembles breadcrumbs.

Stir in the grated cheese, mustard powder and enough milk to form a soft dough.

Knead the dough very lightly on a lightly floured work surface, then flatten it out with the palm of your hand to a depth of about 2.5 cm/1 inch.

Cut the dough into 8 wedges with a knife. Brush the wedges with a little milk and sprinkle with pepper to taste.

Bake in a preheated oven, 220°C/425°F/Gas Mark 7, for 10-15 minutes, until the scones are golden brown.

Transfer the cheese and mustard scones to a wire rack and leave to cool slightly before serving.

Bacon & Polenta Muffins

Ingredients

150 g/5½ oz pancetta

150 g/5½ oz self-raising flour

1 tbsp baking powder

1 tsp salt

250 g/9 oz fine polenta

55 g/2 oz golden granulated sugar

100 g/3½ oz butter, melted

2 eggs, beaten

300 ml/10 fl oz milk

Preheat the oven to 200°C/400°F/Gas Mark 6 and preheat the grill to medium. Line 12 holes of 1 or 2 muffin trays with paper muffin cases. Cook the pancetta under the preheated grill until crisp and then crumble into pieces. Reserve until required.

Sift the flour, baking powder and salt into a bowl, then stir in the polenta and sugar. Place the butter, eggs and milk in a separate bowl. Add the wet ingredients to the dry ingredients and mix until just blended.

Fold in the pancetta, then divide the mixture between the paper cases and bake in the preheated oven for 20-25 minutes, or until risen and golden. Serve the muffins warm or cold.

MAKES: 10

PREP: 15 MINS

COOKING: 20-25 MINS

Cheese Muffins

Ingredients

115 g/4 oz self-raising flour

1 tbsp baking powder

1 tsp salt

225 g/8 oz fine polenta

*150 g/5½ oz grated mature
  Cheddar cheese*

55 g/2 oz butter, melted

2 eggs, beaten

1 garlic clove, crushed

300 ml/10 fl oz milk

Preheat the oven to 200°C/400°F/Gas Mark 6. Line 10 holes of 1 or 2 muffin trays with paper muffin cases. Sift the flour, baking powder and salt into a bowl, then stir in the polenta and 115 g/4 oz of the cheese.

Place the melted butter, eggs, crushed garlic and milk in a separate bowl. Add the wet ingredients to the dry ingredients and mix gently until just combined.

Using a spoon, divide the mixture between the paper cases, scatter over the remaining cheese and bake in the preheated oven for 20-25 minutes, or until risen and golden brown. Serve warm or cold.

Doughnut Muffins

MAKES: 12

PREP: 15 MINS

COOKING: 15-20 MINS

Ingredients

175 g/6 oz butter, softened, plus
  extra for greasing

200 g/7 oz caster sugar

2 large eggs, lightly beaten

375 g/13 oz plain flour

¾ tbsp baking powder

¼ tsp bicarbonate of soda

pinch of salt

½ tsp freshly grated nutmeg

250 ml/9 fl oz milk

TOPPING

100 g/3½ oz caster sugar

1 tsp ground cinnamon

25 g/1 oz butter, melted

Preheat the oven to 180°C/350°F/Gas Mark 4. Grease a deep 12-cup muffin tin.

In a large bowl, beat the butter and sugar together until light and creamy. Add the eggs, a little at a time, beating well between additions.

Sift the flour, baking powder, bicarbonate of soda, salt and nutmeg together. Add half to the creamed mixture with half of the milk. Gently fold the ingredients together before incorporating the remaining flour and milk. Spoon the mixture into the prepared muffin tin, filling each hole to about two-thirds full. Bake for 15-20 minutes, or until the muffins are lightly brown and firm to the touch.

For the topping, mix the sugar and cinnamon together. While the muffins are still warm from the oven, brush lightly with melted butter and sprinkle over the cinnamon and sugar mixture. Eat warm or cold.

Savoury Curried Biscuits

Ingredients

100 g/3½ oz butter, softened, plus extra for greasing

100 g/3½ oz plain flour

1 tsp salt

2 tsp curry powder

100 g/3½ oz Cheshire cheese, grated

100 g/3½ oz Parmesan cheese, freshly grated

Lightly grease about 4 baking trays with a little butter.

Sieve the plain flour and salt into a mixing bowl.

Stir in the curry powder and the grated Cheshire and Parmesan cheeses. Rub in the softened butter with your fingertips until the mixture comes together to form a soft dough.

On a lightly floured surface, roll out the dough thinly to form a rectangle.

Using a 5-cm/2-inch biscuit cutter, cut out 40 round biscuits.

Arrange the biscuits on the prepared baking trays.

Bake in a preheated oven, 180°C/350°F/Gas Mark 4, for 10-15 minutes until golden brown.

Leave the biscuits to cool slightly on the baking trays. Carefully transfer the biscuits to a wire rack and leave until completely cold and crisp, then serve.

Cheese & Rosemary Sables

MAKES: 40

PREP: 15 MINS +
30 MINS
COOLING

COOKING: 10 MINS

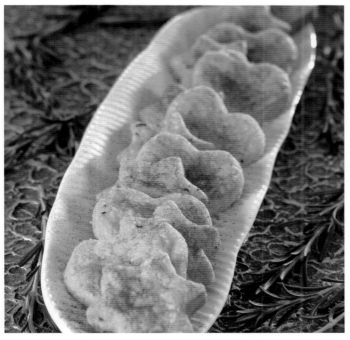

Ingredients

225 g/8 oz cold butter, diced,
plus extra for greasing

250 g/9 oz plain flour

250 g/9 oz grated Gruyère cheese

½ tsp cayenne pepper

2 tsp finely chopped fresh
rosemary leaves

1 egg yolk, beaten with 1 tbsp water

Preheat the oven to 180°C/350°F/Gas Mark 4, then grease 2 baking sheets. Place the flour, butter, cheese, cayenne pepper and rosemary in a food processor. Pulse until the mixture forms a dough, adding a little cold water, if necessary, to bring the mixture together.

On a floured work surface, roll out the pastry to 5 mm/¼ inch thick. Stamp out shapes such as stars and hearts with 6-cm/2½-inch cutters.

Place the shapes on the prepared baking sheets, then cover with clingfilm and leave to chill in the refrigerator for 30 minutes, or until firm. Brush with the beaten egg yolk and bake in the oven for 10 minutes, or until golden brown. Leave to cool on the baking sheets for 2 minutes, then serve warm or transfer to wire racks to cool.

Cheese Straws

MAKES: 24

PREP: 20 MINS +
           30 MINS
           CHILLING

COOKING: 10-15 MINS

Ingredients

115 g/4 oz plain flour, plus extra
  for dusting

pinch of salt

1 tsp curry powder

55 g/2 oz butter, plus
extra for greasing

55 g/2 oz grated Cheddar cheese

1 egg, beaten

poppy and cumin seeds,
  for sprinkling

Sift the flour, salt and curry powder into a bowl. Add the butter and rub in until the mixture resembles breadcrumbs. Add the cheese and half the egg and mix to form a dough. Wrap in clingfilm and chill in the refrigerator for 30 minutes.

Preheat the oven to 200°C/400°F/Gas Mark 6, then grease several baking sheets. On a floured work surface, roll out the dough to 5 mm/¼ inch thick. Cut into 7.5 x 1-cm/3 x ½-inch strips. Pinch the strips lightly along the sides and place on the prepared baking sheets.

Brush the straws with the remaining egg and sprinkle half with poppy seeds and half with cumin seeds. Bake in the preheated oven for 10-15 minutes, or until golden. Transfer to wire racks to cool.

MAKES: 20

PREP: 15 MINS +
45 MINS
CHILLING
(OPTIONAL)

COOKING: 20 MINS

Spiced Cocktail Biscuits

Ingredients

115 g/4 oz butter, plus extra
for greasing

140 g/5 oz plain flour, plus extra
for dusting

2 tsp curry powder

85 g/3 oz grated Cheddar cheese

2 tsp poppy seeds

1 tsp black onion seeds

1 egg yolk

cumin seeds, for sprinkling

Preheat the oven to 190°C/375°F/Gas Mark 5, then grease 2 baking sheets. Sift the flour and curry powder into a bowl. Cut the butter into pieces and add to the flour. Rub in until the mixture resembles breadcrumbs, then stir in the cheese, poppy seeds and black onion seeds. Stir in the egg yolk and mix to a firm dough.

Wrap the dough in clingfilm and chill in the refrigerator for 30 minutes. On a floured work surface, roll out the dough to 3 mm/⅛ inch thick. Stamp out shapes with a cutter. Re-roll the trimmings and stamp out more biscuits until the dough is used up.

Place the biscuits on the prepared baking sheets and sprinkle with the cumin seeds. Leave to chill for a further 15 minutes. Bake in the preheated oven for 20 minutes, or until crisp and golden. Serve warm or transfer to wire racks to cool.

Pesto Palmiers

Ingredients

butter, for greasing

plain flour, for dusting

250 g/9 oz ready-made puff pastry

3 tbsp green or red pesto

1 egg yolk, beaten with 1 tbsp water

25 g/1 oz freshly grated Parmesan cheese

MAKES: 20

PREP: 10 MINS +
          20 MINS
          CHILLING

COOKING: 10 MINS

Preheat the oven to 200°C/400°F/Gas Mark 6, then grease a baking sheet. On a floured work surface, roll out the pastry to a 35 x 15-cm/14 x 6-inch rectangle and trim the edges with a sharp knife. Spread the pesto evenly over the pastry. Roll up the ends tightly to meet in the middle of the pastry.

Wrap in clingfilm and chill in the refrigerator for 20 minutes, until firm, then remove from the refrigerator and unwrap. Brush with the beaten egg yolk on all sides. Cut across into 1-cm/½-inch thick slices. Place the slices on the prepared baking sheet.

Bake in the preheated oven for 10 minutes, or until crisp and golden. Remove from the oven and immediately sprinkle over the Parmesan cheese. Serve the palmiers warm or transfer to a wire rack and leave to cool to room temperature.

Cheese & Peanut Crescents

MAKES: 24

PREP: 10 MINS + 2 HRS CHILLING

COOKING: 15 MINS

Ingredients

425 g/15 oz plain flour, plus extra for dusting

pinch of salt

225 g/8 oz peanut butter

450 g/1 lb hard cheese (e.g. Cheddar or Red Leicester), finely grated

300 g/10½ oz butter or margarine, plus extra for greasing

1 tsp almond essence

DECORATION

mixed nuts, toasted and chopped roughly

icing sugar

In a large bowl, sift together the flour and salt. Add the peanut butter, cheese, butter (or margarine, if using) and almond essence. Mix together until thoroughly combined, then cover with clingfilm and refrigerate for 2 hours.

Preheat the oven to 180°C/350°F/Gas Mark 4. Grease a large baking sheet. Lightly flour a board or work surface. Cut the dough into 24 small pieces and, using your hands, roll each piece into a ball about 2.5 cm/1 inch in diameter. Then roll out each ball into a circle about 3 mm/⅛ inch in thickness. Using a knife, cut a crescent moon out of each circle by removing about a quarter of the dough from each one. Put the crescents onto the baking sheet, transfer to the oven and bake for 15 minutes, or until golden brown.

Remove the cookies from the oven, transfer to a wire rack, sprinkle over the nuts and icing sugar and set aside to cool.

Cheese & Apple Tart

SERVES: 8

PREP: 15 MINS

COOKING: 50 MINS

Ingredients

butter, for greasing

175 g/6 oz self-raising flour

1 tsp baking powder

pinch of salt

75 g/2¾ oz soft brown sugar

100 g/3½ oz stoned dates, chopped

500 g/1lb 2 oz dessert apples, cored and chopped

50 g /1¾ oz walnuts, chopped

60 ml/2 fl oz sunflower oil

2 eggs

175 g/6 oz Red Leicester cheese, grated

Grease a 23-cm/9½-inch loose-bottomed quiche/flan tin and line with baking paper.

Sieve the flour, baking powder and salt into a bowl. Stir in the brown sugar, dates, apples and walnuts. Mix together until well combined.

Beat the oil and eggs together and add the mixture to the dry ingredients. Stir until well combined.

Spoon half of the mixture into the prepared tin and level the surface with the back of a spoon.

Sprinkle with the grated cheese, then spoon over the remaining cake mixture, spreading it evenly to the edges of the tin.

Bake in a preheated oven, 180°C/350°F/Gas Mark 4, for 45-50 minutes or until golden and firm to the touch.

Leave to cool slightly in the tin, then turn out and serve warm.

Festive Feasts

Birthdays, anniversaries, graduation day or Christmas, we all love to

celebrate with something special to eat and, more often than not, the

centrepiece is a truly splendid cake. Festivals and family occasions provide

a wonderful opportunity to show off your home baking skills and this

chapter offers plenty of scope. For example, if you don't have the time or

the confidence to tackle a traditional iced Christmas Cake (see page 124),

why not make a charming but less demanding Yule Log (see page 130)?

Choose from a global array of cakes and desserts – Viennese Sachertorte

(see page 126), Australian Mixed Fruit Pavlova (see page 139) or

Italian Cherry & Chocolate Tiramisu (see page 140).

Don't overlook other traditional baked goodies, whether Hot Cross Buns

(see page 164) and Easter Biscuits (see page 156) for Holy Week,

Festive Mince Pies (see page 150) and Lebkuchen (see page 162) for

Christmas or Party Cookies (see page 158) for any time of year.

Christmas Cake

Ingredients

150 g/5½ oz raisins

125 g/4½ oz stoned dates, chopped

125 g/4½ oz sultanas

100 g/3½ oz glacé cherries, rinsed

150 ml/5 fl oz brandy

225 g/8 oz butter, plus extra
  for greasing

200 g/7 oz caster sugar

4 eggs

grated rind of 1 orange and 1 lemon

1 tbsp black treacle

225 g/8 oz plain flour

½ tsp salt

½ tsp baking powder

1 tsp mixed spice

25 g/1 oz toasted almonds,
  chopped

25 g/1 oz toasted hazelnuts,
  chopped

450 g/1 lb icing sugar

1 egg white

juice of 1 lemon

1 tsp vanilla essence

holly leaves, to decorate

Make this cake at least 3 weeks in advance. Put all the fruit in a bowl, pour over the brandy and soak overnight.

Preheat the oven to 110°C/225°F/Gas Mark ¼. Grease a 20-cm/8-inch cake tin and line it with greaseproof paper. In a bowl, cream together the butter and sugar until fluffy. Gradually beat in the eggs. Stir in the citrus rind and black treacle. In a separate bowl, sift together the flour, salt, baking powder and mixed spice, then fold into the egg mixture. Fold in the fruit, brandy and nuts, then spoon into the cake tin. Bake for at least 3 hours. If it browns too quickly, cover with foil. The cake is cooked when a skewer inserted into the centre comes out clean. Remove from the oven and cool on a wire rack. Store in an airtight container until required.

To make the icing, put the sugar, egg white, lemon juice and vanilla into a bowl and mix until smooth. Spread over the cake, using a fork to give texture. Decorate with holly leaves.

MAKES: 1 (20-CM/ 8-INCH CAKE)

PREP: 45 MINS + 8 HRS SOAKING

COOKING: 3 HRS

Sachertorte

Ingredients

115 g/4 oz unsalted butter,
  softened, plus extra for greasing

175 g/6 oz plain chocolate,
  broken into pieces

3 tbsp black coffee

140 g/5 oz golden caster sugar

5 eggs, separated

140 g/5 oz plain flour, sifted

4 tbsp apricot jam

dash of lemon juice

1 tbsp water

ICING

85 g/3 oz golden caster sugar

4 tbsp water

100 g/3½ oz plain chocolate,
  broken into pieces

Preheat the oven to 160°C/325°F/Gas Mark 3. Grease and line a 23-cm/9-inch round cake tin. Heat the chocolate in a pan with the coffee until melted, stir and cool. Beat the butter and 85 g/3 oz of the sugar in a bowl until fluffy. Beat in the chocolate mixture and egg yolks. Stir in the flour. Whisk the egg whites in a separate bowl until stiff. Whisk in the remaining sugar. Fold into the cake mixture. Turn into the tin and bake for 1–1¼ hours, until firm. Leave in the tin for 5 minutes. Turn out to cool.

Slice the cake in half horizontally. Sandwich together with half the jam. Heat the remaining jam, lemon juice and water in a pan until the jam has melted. Sieve into a bowl. Brush the jam over the top and sides of the cake.

For the icing, heat the sugar and water until boiling and stir until the sugar has dissolved. Remove from the heat, add the chocolate and stir until smooth. Return to the heat and boil to a temperature of 116°C/241°F on a sugar thermometer. Remove from the heat, stir until the mixture stops bubbling, then pour all but 2 tablespoons quickly over the top of the cake, letting it flow down the sides. Smooth round the sides, but do not touch the top. When the icing begins to set, warm the reserved icing and drip the 'Sacher' signature over the top from the tip of a knife.

SERVES: 8-10

PREP: 25 MINS +
2 HRS
SETTING

COOKING: 1 HR 10 MINS-
1 HR 25 MINS

Panforte Di Siena

SERVES: 12-16

PREP: 10 MINS +
20 MINS
COOLING

COOKING: 35-40 MINS

Ingredients

butter, for greasing

55 g/2 oz glacé cherries, quartered

*115 g/4 oz mixed candied orange
and lemon peel, finely chopped*

*25 g/1 oz crystallized ginger,
roughly chopped*

115 g/4 oz flaked almonds

*115 g/4 oz hazelnuts, toasted
and roughly ground*

55 g/2 oz plain flour

25 g/1 oz cocoa powder

1 tsp ground cinnamon

¼ tsp ground cloves

¼ tsp ground nutmeg

¼ tsp ground coriander

115 g/4 oz clear honey

115 g/4 oz golden caster sugar

1 tsp orange flower water

icing sugar, for dusting

Preheat the oven to 160°C/325°F/Gas Mark 3.
Thoroughly grease the base of a 20-cm/8-inch
loose-bottomed cake or flan tin. Line the base with
non-stick baking paper. Place the cherries, candied
peel, ginger, almonds and hazelnuts in a bowl. Sift
in the flour, cocoa powder, cinnamon, cloves, nutmeg
and coriander and mix. Reserve.

Place the honey, sugar and orange flower water in a
saucepan and heat gently until the sugar has dissolved.
Bring the mixture to the boil and boil steadily until a
temperature of 116°C/241°F has been reached on a
sugar thermometer, or a small amount of the mixture
forms a soft ball when dropped into cold water.

Quickly remove the saucepan from the heat and stir in
the dry ingredients. Mix thoroughly and turn into the
prepared tin. Spread evenly and bake in the oven for
30 minutes. Leave to cool in the tin. Turn out and
carefully peel away the lining paper. Dust icing sugar
lightly over the top and cut into wedges to serve.

Yule Log

Ingredients

butter, for greasing

3 eggs

115 g/4 oz golden caster sugar

55 g/2 oz plain flour

25 g/1 oz cocoa powder, plus extra for dusting

Chocolate Caraque

55 g/2 oz white chocolate, melted

icing sugar, for dusting

SYRUP

55 g/2 oz golden caster sugar

150 ml/5 fl oz water

4 tbsp Cointreau

ICING

55 g/2 oz butter, softened

115 g/4 oz icing sugar, sifted

grated rind of 1 orange

1 tbsp Cointreau

BUTTERCREAM

1 tbsp cocoa powder

1 tbsp boiling water

85 g/3 oz butter

175 g/6 oz icing sugar, sifted

Preheat the oven to 200°C/400°F/Gas Mark 6. Grease and line a 20 x 30-cm/8 x 12-inch Swiss roll tin. Whisk the eggs and sugar together until thick and a trail is left when the whisk is lifted. Sift the flour and cocoa powder together into a separate bowl, then fold into the egg mixture. Turn into the tin and bake for 8-10 minutes, or until the cake springs back when lightly pressed. Roll up the sponge and leave to cool.

To make the syrup, heat the sugar and water in a pan until the sugar dissolves. Boil for 2 minutes. Stir in the Cointreau and cool. Unroll the sponge and remove the paper. Sprinkle the sponge with syrup. To make the icing, beat the butter until creamy. Beat in the other ingredients until smooth. Spread over the sponge and roll up.

To make the buttercream, place the cocoa in a heatproof bowl and stir in the water. Cool. Beat the butter in a separate bowl until creamy. Gradually beat in the icing sugar and cocoa until smooth. Cut off a quarter of the roll diagonally and attach to the side of the roll with buttercream. Cover the roll with buttercream and mark lines to represent bark. Cover with Chocolate Caraque (see below). Pipe white chocolate spirals on to the ends. Dust with cocoa and icing sugar and serve.

To make the Chocolate Caraque spread a thin layer of melted chocolate onto a flat surface and just when it appears to have set, but is in fact still soft, hold a knife at a 45° angle to the surface and push it along to form scrolls.

MAKES: 20

PREP: 20 MINS +
1 HR
COOLING/
SETTING

COOKING: 35 MINS

Cup Cakes

Ingredients

200 ml/7 fl oz water

85 g/3 oz butter

85 g/3 oz golden caster sugar

1 tbsp golden syrup

3 tbsp milk

1 tsp vanilla essence

1 tsp bicarbonate of soda

2 tbsp cocoa powder

225 g/8 oz plain flour

ICING

50 g/1¾ oz plain chocolate,
  broken into pieces

4 tbsp water

50 g/1¾ oz butter

50 g/1¾ oz white chocolate,
broken into pieces

350 g/12 oz icing sugar

TO DECORATE

crystallized rose petals

crystallized violets

Preheat the oven to 180°C/350°F/Gas Mark 4. Place paper bun cases in 2 bun tins. Place the water, butter, sugar and syrup in a saucepan. Heat gently, stirring, until the sugar has dissolved, then bring to the boil. Reduce the heat and cook gently for 5 minutes. Remove from the heat and leave to cool. Place the milk and vanilla essence in a bowl. Add the bicarbonate of soda and stir to dissolve. Sift the cocoa powder and flour into a separate bowl and add the syrup mixture. Stir in the milk and beat until smooth.

Carefully spoon the mixture into the paper cases to within two-thirds of the tops. Bake in the oven for 20 minutes, or until well risen and firm to the touch. Leave to cool on a wire rack. To make the icing, place the plain chocolate in a small heatproof bowl with half the water and half the butter and set the bowl over a saucepan of gently simmering water until melted. Stir until smooth and leave over the water. Repeat with the white chocolate and remaining water and butter.

Stir half the icing sugar into each bowl and beat until smooth and fudgy. Divide the icings between the cakes, filling to the top of the paper cases. Leave to cool, then place a crystallized rose petal on each of the plain chocolate iced cakes and a crystallized violet on each white chocolate iced cake. Leave the icing to set before serving.

Giggle Cake

SERVES: 8

PREP: 25 MINS

COOKING: 1 HR 15 MINS

Ingredients

350 g/12 oz mixed dried fruit

125 g/4½ oz butter or margarine,
plus extra for greasing

175 g/6 oz soft brown sugar

225 g/8 oz self-raising flour

pinch of salt

2 eggs, beaten

225 g/8 oz can chopped pineapple,
drained

125 g/4½ oz glacé cherries, halved

Put the mixed dried fruit into a large bowl and cover with boiling water. Set aside to soak for 10-15 minutes, then drain well.

Put the butter or margarine and sugar into a large pan and heat gently until melted. Add the drained mixed dried fruit and cook over a low heat, stirring frequently, for 4-5 minutes. Remove from the heat and transfer to a mixing bowl. Set aside to cool.

Sift together the flour and salt into the dried fruit mixture and stir well. Add the eggs, mixing until the ingredients are thoroughly incorporated.

Add the pineapples and cherries to the cake mixture and stir to combine. Transfer to a greased and lined 1 kg/2 lb loaf tin and level the surface.

Bake in a preheated oven, 180°C/ 350°F/Gas Mark 4, for about 1 hour. Test the cake with a fine skewer; if it comes out clean, the cake is cooked. If not, return to the oven for a few more minutes. Transfer to a wire rack to cool completely before serving.

Spiced Apple Tart

Ingredients

PASTRY

200 g/7 oz plain flour, plus extra for dusting

100 g/3½ oz butter, diced, plus extra for greasing

50 g/1¾ oz icing sugar, sifted

finely grated rind of 1 lemon

1 egg yolk, beaten

3 tbsp milk

FILLING

3 medium cooking apples

2 tbsp lemon juice

finely grated rind of 1 lemon

150 ml/5 fl oz clear honey

175 g/6 oz fresh white or wholemeal breadcrumbs

1 tsp ground mixed spice

pinch of freshly grated nutmeg

whipped cream, to serve

To make the pastry, sift the flour into a bowl. Rub in the butter. Mix in the icing sugar, lemon rind, egg yolk and milk. Knead briefly on a lightly floured work surface, then leave to rest for 30 minutes.

Preheat the oven to 200°C/400°F/Gas Mark 6. Grease a 20-cm/8-inch flan tin with butter. Roll out the pastry to a thickness of 5 mm/¼ inch and use to line the base and sides of the tin.

To make the filling, core 2 apples and grate them into a bowl. Add 1 tablespoon of lemon juice and all the lemon rind, along with the honey, breadcrumbs and mixed spice. Mix together well. Spoon evenly into the pastry shell. Core and slice the remaining apple, and use to decorate the top of the tart. Brush the apple slices with lemon juice, then sprinkle over the nutmeg. Bake in the preheated oven for 35 minutes, or until firm. Remove from the oven and serve with whipped cream.

Dark & White Chocolate Torte

SERVES: 6

PREP: 20 MINS +
            1 HR 20 MINS
            COOLING/
            SETTING

COOKING: 35-40 MINS

Ingredients

butter, for greasing

4 eggs

100 g/3½ oz caster sugar

100 g/3½ oz plain flour

FILLING

300 ml/10 fl oz double cream

150 g/5½ oz plain chocolate, broken into small pieces

TOPPING

75 g/2¾ oz white chocolate

1 tbsp butter

1 tbsp milk

4 tbsp icing sugar

Preheat the oven to 180°C/350°F/Gas Mark 4. Grease and line the base of a 20-cm/8-inch round springform cake tin. Place the eggs and caster sugar in a large bowl and, using an electric whisk, whisk for 10 minutes, or until very light and foamy and the whisk leaves a trail that lasts a few seconds when lifted.

Sift the flour and fold in with a metal spoon or spatula. Pour into the prepared tin and bake in the hot oven for 35-40 minutes, or until springy to the touch. Leave to cool slightly, then transfer to a wire rack to cool completely.

To make the filling, place the cream in a saucepan and bring to the boil, stirring. Add the chocolate and stir until melted. Remove from the heat, transfer to a bowl and cool. Beat until thick.

Slice the cold cake into 2 layers, then sandwich the layers together with the cream. Place on a wire rack.

To make the topping, place the chocolate and butter in a small heatproof bowl and set over a saucepan of simmering water until melted. Stir until blended. Remove from the heat and whisk in the milk, then sift in the icing sugar. Continue whisking for a few minutes until the icing is cool. Pour it over the cake and spread with a spatula to coat the top and sides. Leave to set, then serve.

Raspberry Vacherin

Ingredients

3 egg whites

175 g/6 oz caster sugar

1 tsp cornflour

25 g/1 oz plain chocolate, grated

FILLING

175 g/6 oz plain chocolate

450 ml/16 fl oz double cream, whipped

300 g/10½ oz fresh raspberries

a little melted chocolate, to decorate

Preheat the oven to 140°C/275°F/Gas Mark 1. Draw 3 rectangles, 10 x 25 cm/4 x 10 inches, on sheets of baking paper and place on 2 baking sheets.

Whisk the egg whites in a mixing bowl until soft peaks form, then gradually whisk in half of the sugar and continue whisking until the mixture is very stiff and glossy.

Carefully fold in the rest of the sugar, the cornflour and the grated chocolate with a metal spoon or a palette knife.

Spoon the meringue mixture into a piping bag fitted with a 1-cm/½-inch plain nozzle and pipe lines across the rectangles.

Bake in the preheated oven for 1½ hours, changing the position of the baking sheets halfway through. Without opening the oven door, turn off the oven and leave the meringues to cool inside the oven, then peel away the baking paper.

To make the filling, melt the chocolate and spread it over 2 of the meringue layers. Leave to harden.

Place 1 chocolate-coated meringue on a plate and top with about one-third of the cream and raspberries. Gently place the second chocolate-coated meringue on top and spread with half of the remaining cream and raspberries. Place the last meringue on the top and decorate with the remaining cream and raspberries. Put a few pieces of plain chocolate in a heatproof bowl set over a saucepan of gently simmering water until melted. Drizzle a little melted chocolate over the top of the vacherin and serve.

Mixed Fruit Pavlova

SERVES: 4

PREP: 30 MINS +
30 MINS
COOLING

COOKING: 3 HRS

Ingredients

6 egg whites

pinch of cream of tartar

pinch of salt

275 g/9½ oz caster sugar

600 ml/1 pint double cream

1 tsp vanilla essence

2 kiwi fruits, peeled and sliced

250 g/9 oz strawberries, hulled
and sliced

3 ripe peaches, sliced

1 ripe mango, peeled and sliced

2 tbsp orange liqueur, such
as Cointreau

fresh mint leaves, to decorate

Preheat the oven to 110°C/225°F/Gas Mark ¼.
Line 3 baking sheets with baking paper, then draw a
22-cm/8½-inch circle in the centre of each one. Beat
the egg whites into stiff peaks. Mix in the cream of
tartar and salt. Gradually add 200 g/7 oz of sugar.
Beat for 2 minutes until glossy. Fill a piping bag with
the meringue mixture and pipe enough to fill each
circle, doming them slightly in the centre. Bake for
3 hours. Remove from the oven. Leave to cool.

Whip together the cream and vanilla essence with
75 g/2½ oz of sugar. Put the fruit into a separate bowl
and stir in the liqueur. Put one meringue circle onto a
serving plate, then spread over one-third of the
sugared cream. Spread over one-third of the fruit, then
top with a meringue circle. Spread over another third
of cream, then another third of fruit. Top with the last
meringue circle. Spread over the remaining cream,
followed by the remaining fruit. Decorate with mint
leaves and serve.

139

SERVES: 4

PREP: 20 MINS +
2 HRS
CHILLING

COOKING: NONE

Chocolate & Cherry Tiramisù

Ingredients

200 ml/7 fl oz strong black coffee, cooled to room temperature

6 tbsp cherry brandy

16 trifle sponges

250 g/9 oz mascarpone

300 ml/10 fl oz double cream, lightly whipped

3 tbsp icing sugar

275 g/9½ oz sweet cherries, halved and stoned

60 g/2¼ oz chocolate, curls or grated

whole cherries, to decorate

Pour the cooled coffee into a jug and stir in the cherry brandy. Put half of the trifle sponges into the bottom of a serving dish, then pour over half of the coffee mixture.

Put the mascarpone into a separate bowl along with the cream and sugar and mix together well. Spread half of the mascarpone mixture over the coffee-soaked trifle sponges, then top with half of the cherries. Arrange the remaining trifle sponges on top. Pour over the remaining coffee mixture and top with the remaining cherries. Finish with a layer of mascarpone mixture. Scatter over the grated chocolate, cover with clingfilm, and chill in the refrigerator for at least 2 hours.

Remove from the refrigerator, decorate with cherries and serve.

Profiteroles

SERVES: 4

PREP: 25 MINS

COOKING: 35 MINS

Ingredients

CHOUX PASTRY

5 tbsp butter, plus extra for greasing

200 ml/7 fl oz water

100 g/3½ oz plain flour

3 eggs, beaten

CREAM FILLING

300 ml/10 fl oz double cream

3 tbsp caster sugar

1 tsp vanilla essence

CHOCOLATE & BRANDY SAUCE

125 g/4½ oz plain chocolate, broken into small pieces

2½ tbsp butter

6 tbsp water

2 tbsp brandy

Preheat the oven to 200°C/400°F/Gas Mark 6. Grease a large baking sheet with butter. To make the pastry, put the water and butter into a saucepan and bring to the boil. Meanwhile, sift the flour into a bowl. Remove the pan from the heat and beat in the flour until smooth. Cool for 5 minutes. Beat in enough of the eggs to give the mixture a soft, dropping consistency. Transfer to a piping bag fitted with a 1-cm/½-inch plain nozzle. Pipe small balls onto the baking sheet. Bake for 25 minutes. Remove from the oven. Pierce each ball with a skewer to let steam escape.

To make the filling, whip together the cream, sugar and vanilla essence. Cut the pastry balls almost in half, then fill with cream.

To make the sauce, gently melt the chocolate and butter with the water together in a small saucepan, stirring, until smooth. Stir in the brandy. Pile the profiteroles into individual serving dishes or into a pyramid on a raised cake stand. Pour over the sauce and serve.

Strawberry Chocolate Gâteau

SERVES: 8

PREP: 25 MINS

COOKING: 30-40 MINS

Ingredients

SPONGE

butter, for greasing

3 eggs

115 g/4 oz golden caster sugar

90 g/3¼ oz self-raising flour

2 tbsp cocoa powder

FILLING AND TOPPING

250 g/9 oz strawberries

300 ml/10 fl oz double cream

½ tsp vanilla essence

1 tbsp icing sugar

2 tbsp kirsch

Chocolate Curls

Preheat the oven to 190°C/375°F/Gas Mark 5. Grease and line a 22-cm/8½-inch cake tin. To make the sponge, place the eggs and sugar in a bowl and whisk until thick and mousse-like and a trail is left when the whisk is lifted. Sift the flour and cocoa powder into a separate bowl, then fold into the whisked mixture. Turn into the tin and bake in the oven for 30-40 minutes, or until the cake springs back when pressed in the centre. Leave in the tin for 5 minutes, then turn out on to a wire rack to cool.

Meanwhile, prepare the filling. Reserve 4 strawberries and hull and slice the remainder. Whip the cream, vanilla essence and icing sugar together until thick. Reserve two-thirds of the cream and fold the strawberries into the remainder.

Slice the sponge horizontally into 2 layers and sprinkle each layer with 1 tablespoon of kirsch. Place one layer on a serving plate and spread over the strawberry cream mixture. Place the other sponge layer on top. Place some of the reserved cream mixture in a piping bag fitted with a fluted nozzle and spread the remainder over the top and sides of the cake. Coat the sides with Chocolate Curls. Pipe the cream round the top of the cake. Cut the reserved strawberries in half, keeping the stalks intact, and arrange on the piped cream.

144

Baked Chocolate Alaska

SERVES: 4

PREP: 50 MINS

COOKING: 12 MINS

Ingredients

butter, for greasing

2 eggs

4 tbsp caster sugar

5 tbsp plain flour

2 tbsp cocoa powder

3 egg whites

150 g/5½ oz caster sugar

*1 litre/1¾ pints good-quality
chocolate ice cream*

Preheat the oven to 220°C/425°F/Gas Mark 7. Grease an 18-cm/7-inch round cake tin with butter and line the base with baking paper.

Whisk the eggs and the 4 tablespoons of sugar in a bowl until very thick and pale. Sift the flour and cocoa powder together and fold in.

Pour into the prepared tin and bake in the preheated oven for 7 minutes, or until springy to the touch. Transfer to a wire rack to cool.

Whisk the egg whites in a spotlessly clean, greasefree bowl until soft peaks form. Gradually add the sugar, whisking, until you have a thick, glossy meringue.

Place the sponge on a large baking tray and pile the ice cream in the centre in a heaped dome.

Pipe or spread the meringue over the ice cream, making sure that the ice cream is completely enclosed. (At this point the dessert can be frozen, if you like.)

Return to the oven for 5 minutes, or until the meringue is just golden. Serve immediately.

Mincemeat & Grape Jalousie

SERVES: 4

PREP: 1 HR 15 MINS

COOKING: 45 MINS

Ingredients

1 tbsp butter, for greasing

plain flour, for dusting

*500 g/1lb 2 oz fresh ready-made
puff pastry, thawed if frozen*

410 g/14½ oz mincemeat

*100 g/3½ oz grapes, deseeded
and halved*

1 egg, lightly beaten, for glazing

demerara sugar, for sprinkling

Lightly grease a baking tray with the butter.

Roll out the pastry on a lightly floured work surface, and cut it into 2 rectangles.

Place 1 pastry rectangle on the prepared baking tray and brush the edges with a little water.

Mix the mincemeat and grapes together in a mixing bowl. Spread the mixture over the pastry rectangle on the baking tray, leaving a 2.5-cm/1-inch border.

Fold the second pastry rectangle in half lengthways and carefully cut a series of parallel lines across the folded edge with a sharp knife, leaving a 2.5-cm/1-inch border.

Open out the pastry rectangle and lay it over the mincemeat, then press the edges of the pastry firmly together to seal.

Flute and crimp the edges of the pastry with your fingertips. Lightly brush with the beaten egg and sprinkle with a little demerara sugar.

Bake the jalousie in a preheated oven, 220°C/425°F/ Gas Mark 7, for 15 minutes. Reduce the heat to 180°C/350°F/Gas Mark 4 and cook for a further 30 minutes, until the jalousie is well risen and golden brown.

Transfer the jalousie to a wire rack to cool completely before serving.

Festive Mince Pies

MAKES: 12

PREP: 20 MINS

COOKING: 15 MINS

Ingredients

200 g/7 oz plain flour, plus extra for dusting

100 g/3½ oz butter

25 g/1 oz icing sugar

1 egg yolk

2-3 tbsp milk

300 g/10½ oz mincemeat

1 egg, beaten, for sealing and glazing

icing sugar, for dusting

sprigs of holly, to decorate

Preheat the oven to 180°C/350°F/Gas Mark 4. Sift the flour into a mixing bowl. Using your fingertips, rub in the butter until the mixture resembles breadcrumbs. Mix in the sugar and egg yolk. Stir in enough milk to make a soft dough, turn out onto a lightly floured work surface and knead lightly until smooth.

Shape the dough into a ball and roll out to a thickness of 1 cm/½ inch. Use fluted cutters to cut out 12 rounds of 7 cm/2¾ inches diameter and 12 rounds of 5 cm/2 inches diameter. Dust 12 tartlet tins with flour and line with the larger dough rounds. Prick the bases with a fork, then half-fill each pie with mincemeat. Brush beaten egg around the rims, then press the smaller dough rounds on top to seal. Make a small hole in the top of each one. Decorate the pies with Christmas trees made from dough trimmings. Brush all over with beaten egg, then bake for 15 minutes. Remove from the oven and cool on a wire rack. Dust with icing sugar, decorate and serve.

151

Double Chocolate Chip Cookies

MAKES: 24

PREP: 15 MINS +
          20 MINS
          COOLING

COOKING: 10-15 MINS

Ingredients

115 g/4 oz butter, softened, plus
  extra for greasing

55 g/2 oz golden granulated sugar

55 g/2 oz light muscovado sugar

1 egg, beaten

½ tsp vanilla essence

115 g/4 oz plain flour

2 tbsp cocoa powder

½ tsp bicarbonate of soda

115 g/4 oz milk chocolate chips

55 g/2 oz walnuts, roughly chopped

Preheat the oven to 180°C/350°F/Gas Mark 4, then grease 3 baking sheets. Place the butter, granulated sugar and muscovado sugar in a bowl and beat until light and fluffy. Gradually beat in the egg and vanilla essence.

Sift the flour, cocoa and bicarbonate of soda into the mixture and stir in carefully. Stir in the chocolate chips and walnuts. Drop dessertspoonfuls of the mixture on to the prepared baking sheets, spaced well apart to allow for spreading.

Bake in the oven for 10-15 minutes, or until the mixture has spread and the cookies are beginning to feel firm. Leave to cool on the baking sheets for 2 minutes, then transfer to wire racks to cool completely.

Traditional Spiced Cookies

Ingredients

215 g/7½ oz plain flour

2 tsp mixed spice

1 tsp salt

1 tsp bicarbonate of soda

175 g/6 oz butter or margarine,
plus extra for greasing

100 g/3½ oz granulated sugar

200 g/7 oz light muscovado sugar,
plus extra for dusting

2 eggs

4 tbsp milk

300 g/10½ oz rolled oats

75 g/2¾ oz raisins

75 g/2¾ oz sultanas

Mix the flour, mixed spice, salt and bicarbonate of soda together and sift into a large mixing bowl.

One at a time, mix in the butter (or margarine, if using), both sugars, the eggs and the milk. Beat the mixture until it is smooth.

Add the oats and dried fruit and stir thoroughly. Cover the bowl with clingfilm and place it in the refrigerator to chill for 1 hour.

Preheat the oven to 190°C/375°F/Gas Mark 5 and grease a large baking sheet.

Put 36 tablespoonfuls of cookie mixture onto the greased baking sheet, making sure they are well spaced. Dust lightly with muscovado sugar. Transfer to the preheated oven and bake for 12 minutes, or until the cookies are golden brown.

Remove the cookies from the oven and place on a wire rack to cool thoroughly.

Mincemeat Crumble Bars

MAKES:	12
PREP:	20 MINS + 1 HR CHILLING/ COOLING
COOKING:	32-35 MINS

Ingredients

400 g/14 oz ready-made mincemeat

icing sugar, for dusting

BASE

140 g/5 oz butter, plus
extra for greasing

85 g/3 oz golden caster sugar

140 g/5 oz plain flour

85 g/3 oz cornflour

TOPPING

115 g/4 oz self-raising flour

85 g/3 oz butter, cut into pieces

85 g/3 oz golden caster sugar

25 g/1 oz flaked almonds

Grease a shallow 28 x 20-cm/11 x 8-inch cake tin. To make the base, place the butter and sugar in a bowl and cream together until light and fluffy. Sift in the flour and cornflour and, with your hands, bring the mixture together to form a ball. Push the dough into the prepared tin, pressing it out and into the corners with your fingers, then leave to chill in the refrigerator for 20 minutes. Preheat the oven to 200°C/400°F/Gas Mark 6. After chilling, bake the base in the oven for 12-15 minutes, or until puffed and golden.

To make the crumble topping, place the flour, butter and sugar in a bowl and rub together to form rough crumbs. Stir in the almonds.

Spread the mincemeat over the base and scatter the crumbs on top. Bake in the oven for a further 20 minutes, or until golden brown. Leave to cool slightly, then cut into 12 pieces and leave to cool completely. Dust with sifted icing sugar, then serve.

Easter Biscuits

MAKES: 24

PREP: 20 MINS +
20 MINS
COOLING

COOKING: 10-15 MINS

Ingredients

175 g/6 oz butter, softened, plus
extra for greasing

175 g/6 oz golden caster sugar

1 egg, beaten

2 tbsp milk

55 g/2 oz chopped mixed peel

115 g/4 oz currants

350 g/12 oz plain flour, plus extra
for dusting

1 tsp mixed spice

GLAZE

1 egg white, lightly beaten

2 tbsp golden caster sugar

Preheat the oven to 180°C/350°F/Gas Mark 4, then grease 2 large baking sheets. Place the butter and sugar in a bowl and beat until light and fluffy. Gradually beat in the egg and milk. Stir in the mixed peel and currants, then sift in the flour and mixed spice. Mix together to make a firm dough. Knead lightly until smooth.

On a floured work surface, roll out the dough to 5 mm/¼ inch thick and use a 5-cm/2-inch round biscuit cutter to stamp out the biscuits. Re-roll the dough trimmings and stamp out more biscuits until the dough is used up. Place the biscuits on the prepared baking sheets and bake in the preheated oven for 10 minutes.

Remove from the oven to glaze. Brush with the egg white and sprinkle with the caster sugar, then return to the oven for a further 5 minutes, or until lightly browned. Leave to cool on the baking sheets for 2 minutes, then transfer to wire racks to cool completely.

Party Cookies

MAKES: 16

PREP: 10 MINS +
           20 MINS
           COOLING

COOKING: 10-12 MINS

Ingredients

115 g/4 oz butter, softened, plus extra for greasing

115 g/4 oz light muscovado sugar

1 tbsp golden syrup

½ tsp vanilla essence

175 g/6 oz self-raising flour

85 g/3 oz sugar-coated chocolate beans

Preheat the oven to 180°C/350°F/Gas Mark 4, then grease 2 baking sheets. Place the butter and sugar in a bowl and beat together with an electric whisk until light and fluffy, then beat in the syrup and vanilla essence.

Sift in half the flour and work it into the mixture. Stir in the chocolate beans and the remaining flour and work the dough together with your fingers.

Roll out the dough into 16 balls and place them on the prepared baking sheets, spaced well apart to allow for spreading. Do not flatten them. Bake in the preheated oven for 10-12 minutes, or until pale golden at the edges. Remove from the oven and leave to cool on the baking sheets for 2 minutes, then transfer to wire racks to cool completely.

Christmas Shortbread

MAKES: 24

PREP: 30 MINS +
10-15 MINS
CHILLING

COOKING: 10-15 MINS

Ingredients

125 g/4½ oz caster sugar

*225 g/8 oz butter, plus extra
for greasing*

*350 g/12 oz plain flour, sifted,
plus extra for dusting*

pinch of salt

TO DECORATE

55 g/2 oz icing sugar

silver balls

glacé cherries

angelica

Beat the sugar and butter together in a large bowl until combined (thorough creaming is not necessary).

Sift in the flour and salt and work together to form a stiff dough. Turn out on to a lightly floured work surface. Knead lightly for a few moments until smooth, but avoid over-handling. Chill in the refrigerator for 10-15 minutes. Preheat the oven to 180°C/350°F/Gas Mark 4. Grease several baking sheets.

Roll out the dough on a lightly floured work surface and cut into shapes with small Christmas cutters, such as trees, bells, stars and angels. Place on greased baking sheets.

Bake in the oven for 10-15 minutes, until pale golden brown. Leave to cool on the baking sheets for 10 minutes, then transfer to wire racks to cool completely.

Mix the icing sugar with a little water to make a glacé icing, and use to ice the biscuits. Before the icing sets, decorate with silver balls, tiny pieces of glacé cherries and angelica. Store in an airtight container or wrap the biscuits individually in cellophane, tie with coloured ribbon or string, then hang them on the Christmas tree as edible decorations.

Lebkuchen

Ingredients

3 eggs

200 g/7 oz golden caster sugar

55 g/2 oz plain flour

2 tsp cocoa powder

1 tsp ground cinnamon

½ tsp ground cardamom

¼ tsp ground cloves

¼ tsp ground nutmeg

175 g/6 oz ground almonds

*55 g/2 oz mixed candied peel,
  chopped finely*

TO DECORATE

115 g/4 oz plain chocolate

115 g/4 oz white chocolate

sugar crystals

Preheat the oven to 180°C/350°F/Gas Mark 4.
Line several baking sheets with non-stick baking paper.
Put the eggs and sugar in a heatproof bowl set over a
saucepan of gently simmering water. Whisk until thick
and foamy. Remove the bowl from the saucepan and
continue to whisk for 2 minutes.

Sift the flour, cocoa, cinnamon, cardamom, cloves and
nutmeg into the bowl and stir in with the ground
almonds and chopped peel. Drop heaped teaspoonfuls
of the mixture on to the prepared baking sheets,
spreading them gently into smooth mounds.

Bake in the oven for 15-20 minutes, until light brown
and slightly soft to the touch. Cool on the baking sheets
for 10 minutes, then transfer to wire racks to cool
completely. Put the plain and white chocolate in
2 separate heatproof bowls set over 2 saucepans of
gently simmering water until melted. Dip half the
biscuits in melted plain chocolate and half in white.
Sprinkle with sugar crystals and leave to set.

Yuletide Cookies

Ingredients

350 g/12 oz self-raising flour,
  plus extra for dusting

1 tsp bicarbonate of soda

1 tbsp powdered ginger

3 tsp mixed spice

pinch of salt

125 g/4½ oz butter or margarine,
  plus extra for greasing

5 tbsp golden syrup

200 g/7 oz demerara sugar

1 egg

1 tsp brandy

1 tsp very finely grated orange zest

icing sugar, to decorate

MAKES: 24

PREP: 20 MINS +
          4 HRS
          CHILLING

COOKING: 10 MINS

In a large bowl, sift together the flour, bicarbonate of soda, ginger, mixed spice and salt. In a separate bowl, beat together the butter (or margarine, if using), golden syrup, sugar, egg and brandy until thoroughly combined. Gradually stir in the grated orange zest, then the flour mixture.

Halve the dough, then wrap in clingfilm and refrigerate for at least 4 hours (it will keep for up to 6 days). When ready to use, preheat the oven to 350°F/180°C/Gas Mark 4 and grease a baking sheet.

Flour a board or work surface. Roll each half of dough into a ball, then roll it to a thickness of 3 mm/⅛ inch. Using cookie cutters or a knife, cut festive shapes such as stars and trees. Put the cookies onto the greased baking sheet, transfer to the oven and bake for 10 minutes, or until golden brown. Remove the cookies from the oven, transfer to a wire rack and set aside. When the cookies have cooled completely, drizzle over the icing sugar and serve.

163

Hot Cross Buns

Ingredients

500 g/1 lb 2 oz strong white
  bread flour, plus extra for dusting

½ tsp salt

2 tsp ground mixed spice

1 tsp ground nutmeg

1 tsp ground cinnamon

2 tsp easy-blend dried yeast

50 g/1¾ oz golden caster sugar

finely grated rind of 1 lemon

175 g/6 oz currants

75 g/2¾ oz chopped mixed peel

75 g/2¾ oz butter, melted

1 egg

225 ml/7½ fl oz tepid milk

vegetable oil, for brushing

CROSSES

50 g/1¾ oz plain flour

25 g/1 oz butter, cut into pieces

1 tbsp cold water

GLAZE

3 tbsp milk

3 tbsp golden caster sugar

Sift the flour, salt and spices into a bowl and stir in the yeast, sugar, lemon rind, currants and mixed peel. Make a well in the centre. In a separate bowl, mix the melted butter, egg and milk. Pour into the dry ingredients and mix to make a soft dough, adding more milk if necessary. Brush a bowl with oil. Turn the dough out on to a floured work surface and knead for 10 minutes, or until smooth and elastic. Place the dough in the oiled bowl, cover with clingfilm and leave in a warm place for 1¾-2 hours, or until doubled in size.

Turn out on to a floured work surface, knead for 1-2 minutes, then divide into 12 balls. Place on a greased baking sheet, flatten slightly, then cover with oiled clingfilm. Leave in a warm place for 45 minutes, or until doubled in size. Preheat the oven to 220°C/425°F/Gas Mark 7.

To make the crosses, sift the flour into a bowl and rub in the butter. Stir in the cold water to make a dough. Divide into 24 strips, 18 cm/7 inches long. To make the glaze, place the milk and sugar in a saucepan over a low heat and stir until the sugar has dissolved. Brush some of the glaze over the buns and lay the pastry strips on them to form crosses. Bake in the oven for 15-20 minutes, or until golden. Brush with the remaining glaze and return to the oven for 1 minute. Cool on a wire rack.

MAKES: 12

PREP: 35 MINS +
            2 HRS 45 MINS
            RISING

COOKING: 16-21 MINS

SERVES: 8

PREP: 25 MINS +
1 HR
COOLING

COOKING: 1 HR 10 MINS

Cinnamon & Currant Loaf

Ingredients

*150 g/5½ oz butter, cut into
small pieces, plus extra
for greasing*

350 g/12 oz plain flour

pinch of salt

1 tbsp baking powder

1 tbsp ground cinnamon

125 g/4½ oz soft brown sugar

175 g/6 oz currants

finely grated rind of 1 orange

5-6 tbsp orange juice

6 tbsp milk

2 eggs, lightly beaten

Preheat the oven to 180°C/350°F/Gas Mark 4.
Grease a 900-g/2-lb loaf tin and line the base with
baking paper.

Sift the flour, salt, baking powder and cinnamon into a
large bowl. Rub in the butter pieces with your fingers
until the mixture resembles coarse breadcrumbs.

Stir in the sugar, currants and orange rind. Beat the
orange juice, milk and eggs together and add to the
dry ingredients. Mix well. Spoon the mixture into
the tin and make a slight dip in the centre to help it
rise evenly.

Bake in the preheated oven for 1-1 hour 10 minutes,
or until a fine metal skewer inserted into the centre of
the loaf comes out clean. Leave the loaf to cool in the
tin for 10 minutes, then turn out on to a wire rack to
cool completely before slicing and serving.

Crown Loaf

Ingredients

2 tbsp butter, cut into small pieces,
 plus extra for greasing

225 g/8 oz strong white bread flour

½ tsp salt

1 sachet easy-blend dried yeast

125 ml/4 fl oz hand-hot milk

1 egg, beaten

FILLING

4 tbsp butter, softened

50 g/1¾ oz soft brown sugar

25 g/1 oz chopped hazelnuts

25 g/1 oz stem ginger, chopped

50 g/1¾ oz mixed peel

1 tbsp rum or brandy

100 g/3½ oz icing sugar

2 tbsp lemon juice

Grease a baking sheet. Sieve the flour and salt into a bowl. Stir in the yeast. Rub in the butter with your fingers. Add the milk and egg and mix to a dough.

Place the dough in a greased bowl, cover and leave in a warm place for 40 minutes until doubled in size. Knead the dough lightly for 1 minute to knock it back. Roll out to a rectangle 30 x 23 cm/12 x 9 inches.

To make the filling, cream together the butter and sugar until the mixture is light and fluffy. Stir in the hazelnuts, ginger, mixed peel and rum or brandy. Spread the filling over the dough, leaving a 2.5-cm/ 1-inch border.

Roll up the dough, starting from the long edge, to form a sausage shape. Cut the dough roll into slices at 5-cm/2-inch intervals and place on the baking tray in a circle with the slices just touching. Cover and set aside to rise in a warm place for 30 minutes.

Bake in a preheated oven, 190°C/325°F/Gas Mark 5, for 20-30 minutes or until golden. Meanwhile, mix the icing sugar with enough lemon juice to form a thin icing.

Leave the loaf to cool slightly before drizzling with icing. Allow the icing to set slightly before serving the loaf.

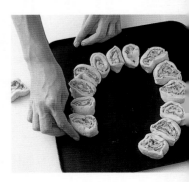

Stollen

SERVES: 10

PREP: 30 MINS +
5 HRS
RISING

COOKING: 40 MINS

Ingredients

85 g/3 oz currants

55 g/2 oz raisins

30 g/1⅛ oz chopped mixed peel

*55 g/2 oz glacé cherries, rinsed,
dried and quartered*

2 tbsp rum

55 g/2 oz butter

175 ml/6 fl oz milk

25 g/1 oz golden caster sugar

*375 g/13 oz strong white bread
flour, plus extra for dusting*

½ tsp ground nutmeg

½ tsp ground cinnamon

seeds from 3 cardamoms

2 tsp easy-blend dried yeast

finely grated rind of 1 lemon

1 egg, beaten

40 g/1½ oz flaked almonds

vegetable oil, for brushing

175 g/6 oz marzipan

melted butter, for brushing

sifted icing sugar, for dredging

Place the currants, raisins, peel and cherries in a bowl, stir in the rum and reserve. Place the butter, milk and sugar in a saucepan over a low heat and stir until the sugar dissolves and the butter melts. Cool until hand-hot. Sift the flour, nutmeg and cinnamon into a bowl. Crush the cardamom seeds and add them. Stir in the yeast. Make a well in the centre, stir in the milk mixture, lemon rind and egg and beat into a dough.

Turn the dough out on to a floured work surface. Knead for 5 minutes, adding more flour if necessary. Knead in the soaked fruit and the almonds. Transfer to a clean, oiled bowl. Cover with clingfilm and leave in a warm place for up to 3 hours, or until doubled in size. Turn out on to a floured surface, knead for 1-2 minutes, then roll out to a 25-cm/10-inch square.

Roll the marzipan into a sausage slightly shorter than the length of the dough. Place down the centre. Fold the dough over to cover the marzipan, overlapping it, and seal the ends. Place seam-side down on a greased baking sheet, cover with oiled clingfilm and leave in a warm place for up to 2 hours, or until doubled in size. Preheat the oven to 190°C/375°F/Gas Mark 5. Bake for 40 minutes, or until golden and hollow-sounding when tapped. Brush with melted butter, dredge with icing sugar and cool on a wire rack.

Special Day Bakes

Entertaining friends and family is great when everything goes with a swing, but can be quite hectic and stressful to plan and prepare. Before you start, it's worth reminding yourself that your guests will really appreciate your freshly-baked treats from the moment they arrive and smell the tantalising aroma coming from your kitchen. They'll be concentrating on the delights of good home baking and certainly won't be marking your achievements on a score card.

There are two main guidelines for success – don't be too ambitious and plan well in advance, down to the smallest detail. Always choose something you are confident about making and be realistic about your time. A frazzled wreck who has been up half the night making pastry or whisking egg whites is never going to be the hostess with the mostest!

This section gives some ideas for four occasions and can be easily adapted for most social gatherings.

Morning Coffee **with Friends**

Fresh Croissants
p 96-97

Coffee Streusel Cake
p 16-17

Cappuccino Squares
p 55

Classic Oatmeal Cookies
p 38-39

Afternoon Tea **with the Family**

Cherry Scones
p 76

Rich Fruit Cake
p 22-23

Victoria Sandwich Cake
p 12-13

Chelsea Buns
p 77

Kids' Party Time

Gingerbread People
p 46-47

Party Cookies
p 158-159

Triple Chocolate Muffins
p 36

Lemon Butterfly Cakes
p 48-49

An Occasion to Impress

Cheese Straws
p 114-115

Banoffee Pie
p 65

Manhattan Cheesecake
p 66-67

Strawberry Chocolate Gâteau
p 144-145

INDEX